THE FREEDOM PROJECT

THE FREEDOM PROJECT

TRAVEL

WILKO VAN DE KAMP

DYNAMIC WINDMILL

Published by:
Dynamic Windmill, PO Box 2751 Stn. M, Calgary, Alberta, T2P 3C2, Canada
www.dynamicwindmill.com

Ordering Information - Quantity sales
Special discounts are available on quantity purchases by corporations, associations, and others. For details, contact the publisher.

ISBN 978-0-9938260-0-9

First Edition

For all the remarkable people who crossed
the path of my journey through life on earth.
Life is made by the people you travel with.

Contents

Come Home   *157*

Why I wrote this book

After traveling over a large portion of the world well before the age of thirty the travel bug really got to me. It caught me by surprise, as traveling wasn't something I was used to while growing up. I don't think I crossed any borders as a child. My first international travels were probably the trips I took to France and Germany in my early twenties. That sounds pretty exotic from a North American perspective, but since I grew up in Europe those were mostly short day trips by car. After my first plane trip to one of the Spanish islands I realized how much I loved traveling. I started to do more and more of it: both personally, and later on even for work. By now, I think it's safe to say I've seen some of the most beautiful places of this earth, and a lot remains to be explored on future travels. There's always something new to see, and I'm surprised how I discover a new favorite place on every trip.

A couple of months ago, just before starting to write this book, I went on a trip of a lifetime to Asia. The schedule was jam-packed with many different countries. Since I had never been to Asia before, it seemed like a great idea to cover as much terrain as possible. Japan, China, Malaysia and various islands of the Philippines were all part of the four week itinerary. As with any trip, I've seen some amazing things, and I was taken well out of my comfort zone by being confronted with cultures and languages that were completely foreign to me. Putting it black and white, the trip also turned out to be a one-month executive summary of how *not* to travel. Despite all the beautiful things I saw in Asia, practically speaking there were a lot of things that I had done completely different on previous travels. Without knowing it, I had experimented a lot with different types of travel over the years. Subconsciously I had formed some "best practices" about traveling that I had already started to follow for years. Step by step I had educated myself on how to travel. What to do, what not to do, and how to go about doing it. I never realized it might be harder than it seems to get this concept of traveling right. If anything, my trip of a lifetime to Asia has made me finally become aware of some of those travel principles I had subconsciously formed. Quite the wake up call, and one of the two reasons that made me decide to write this book. I'm looking forward to share some of those travel "best practices" I formed with you. I'll retrieve them one by one from my subconscious mind, write them down, and share them with you. Not as a step-by-step instruction manual with laws set in stone about how "thou shalt" organize all your future trips, but more as a set of practical, useful guidelines that you can use when and where you need them. Use this book at your leisure, literally.

The second, and main reason to write this book, is my desire to motivate you to book that trip you've been thinking about for some time now. Being a travel photographer I exhibit my work that I have for sale at various art shows and events. While pondering over the pictures, people often say, "I've always wanted to go there". My pictures from Paris, New York and Buenos Aires seem to be quite popular and invoke that reaction without exception, in people of all ages. It makes me a little sad sometimes. I know it's not

> *"The World is a book,*
> *and those who do not*
> *travel read only a page"*
>
> *Ernest Hemingway*

as simple as responding with "so why don't you go", or "why haven't you gone yet". There are all sorts of reasons as to why it's not that easy: responsibilities at home, a demanding career, or financial reasons. After all, travel isn't cheap, right? But regardless of all those excuses and limiting circumstances, there's (at least) that one place in the back of your mind that you've always wanted to see, but never did. The one you're thinking about right now. Am I right? I hope to encourage you to make what might seem to be a difficult decision, and just go for it. Not to ignore, but to overcome, and find solutions for all those reasons that might have discouraged you from packing your bags, to go explore, dream, and live your life.

I'm going to share some practical advice that will give you the tools to overcome at least a few of those limiting circumstances. I wouldn't call myself a travel guru, but there are some mysteries in the world of travel that I will unravel in this book. I will share some of the "secrets" with you that surround the concept of travel. One thing I've learned is that it's not that hard to just pack up your things and go. In my life, I've left literally everything behind that I was familiar with, on more than one occasion. While it seemed very scary and risky at the time, it has *always* paid off, although sometimes in different ways than I expected or had planned for. If anything, I hope this book will inspire you to just go - and give you some of the tools and inspiration to show you it's really not that hard. Just place one foot before the other, and repeat that motion, step by step. Anyone can do it. The wonderful, enriching experience of travel is for everyone. After all, travel is the only thing you can buy that will make you richer: there are amazing benefits to be had from exploring the world; benefits that you will take home to your day-to-day life. They will enrich and inspire you, creating an opportunity to build your entire life based on the feeling of freedom travel has brought you. So go on, allow yourself to book that trip, and to explore this wonderful planet we live on. You already know where you want to go.

How to use this book

I've structured this book around the most significant phases in the process of travel. They form the seven steps I always go through when I'm going on a trip, whether it's a business trip to a different city or a vacation to some remote beach destination.

1. Escape

What are your reasons *not* to travel? Do life and passion get in the way, or is it more a time and money thing? Something to save for retirement maybe?

2. Plan

Where do you want to go, and how long do you need to stay there to get the most out of the trip? And what are you looking to get out of the trip in the first place?

3. Book

What's the best way to book a trip? Do you book direct, or with the help of a travel agent or tour operator? How do you go about booking airfare, and is it actually possible to fly for free?

4. Prepare

How do you prepare for a trip? What to pack, and how to deal with baggage restrictions and overweight charges? Do you need foreign currency? What to do in case of trouble while traveling?

5. Go there

What is the most important thing to focus on while traveling? How do you turn the entire trip into a pleasant experience, especially when dealing with airports, long-haul flights and jet lag?

6. Be there

How do you really get the most out of any trip - from the very first meal until spending your last cash on souvenirs before returning home? Where do you eat? How to stay safe while traveling? What should you not do while on a trip?

7. Come home

Why is our traveling self so different from the person we are at home? Is it possible to take the liberating experience of travel as a mental souvenir and apply it right where we live?

Over the course of this book I'll also introduce you to two of the guiding principles that I use throughout all of these steps: *Experience Value* and *Small Victories*. Combined, those are the essential tools to make any trip enjoyable - from the moment you pack your bags and head to the airport until you come back home and do laundry after days, weeks or even months of roaming the world.

You don't necessarily need to read this book from cover to cover to benefit from the tips I share. If you currently have no concrete plans for any travel you might as well start at the beginning, but if you've already booked a trip you can follow the process from where you left off by diving right into the chapter that would be the next step in your travel experience. For example, if you've already booked a flight and hotel for your next trip feel free to dive right into chapter three which talks about further preparations for your trip. If you read this book just before departure or when already at the airport or maybe even onboard of that long-haul flight, feel free to skip to chapter four or five to get the most out of your trip right away, and re-read the other chapters later to help prepare for your next trip.

In addition to the book there are also bonus resources available online with links to useful websites and additional content. Nothing changes as much as the world of the internet, so to prevent me from including a collection of outdated links printed in this book that might no longer work in future, I'm adding all extra resources to the web page of this book:

www.dynamicwindmill.com/the-freedom-project

Now, as John Muir said, "the mountains are calling and I must go". So I'll leave you to enjoy this book, and start on your own freedom project. Enjoy the experience!

Wilko van de Kamp
Calgary - July 2014

ESCAPE

WHAT GETS IN THE WAY OF GETTING AWAY?

Moments

E ver had a moment, or more, where you want to just get up, walk out the door, get in your car, board a random airplane and not even care where you'll end up? Do you wish you could shrink the world to make certain cities closer to each other, and easier to travel to? Are you ready, or maybe even long overdue for a vacation to a place you've never been? You don't need a winning lottery ticket to get there. Allow me to show you how.

Let's consider some of the reasons not to travel first, as there are lots of them. Some people simply have no desire to leave their hometown. If that's the case there's probably very little this book will do for you, unless you're looking for a major change in your lifestyle. But even if there's a burning desire to travel, I've heard many reasons to not leave home.

Pointing at one's life partner: "He won't let me." Or, "She won't let me."

"My finances don't allow me. I have a mortgage payment, car payment, and credit card payment. At the end of my money there's always some bills left to pay."

"We have young children and can't possibly travel. It's too much of a hassle, and too expensive."

"It's way too dangerous to travel these days. Bad things happen in the world constantly."

"I can't get the time off from work, and even if I could get a few days off, I'm just too busy and will never get my work done."

The list goes on. Most reasons people have to not travel are just excuses, that keep us trapped in circumstances that we think are comfortable. It's nice to stay inside the boundaries of that comfort zone, whatever we make it out to be. Blaming something external like a job, life partner or the kids is a convenient way to avoid taking *full* responsibility for our own life, and having to question those "comforts" too much for comfort.

Fear of traveling, or fear of going outside of our comfort zone, is perfectly normal. But fear is often based on perception, some idea we have in the back of our minds. Even though most of those ideas are not based on reality, I still use them as leverage to do some risk-mitigation planning. I don't shy away from asking myself the tough questions to see what the absolute worst is that could happen. It turns out that most risks can be avoided, and aside from a few exceptions, most decisions I make today can be reversed later on, if I decide to take on a different path.

Life won't fall apart if you take two weeks off. As a matter of fact it might actually improve. Sometimes those who wander off end up having the greatest adventures. So go on, explore. Allow yourself to book that trip to that one place you've always wanted to go. You deserve it. But you don't really need me to tell you that - you need to believe it yourself. Travel often. Getting lost will help you find yourself.

Life and passion

A healthy work life balance is important. Even job advertisements talk about how the company I'm about to work for will "allow" for a great work - life balance. Which is really nice of them. Because when I deduct the hours in a twenty-four hour day I spend sleeping, the majority of the remainder of that time I'll end up spending in the confines of the office. Turns out the promised work - life balance isn't much of a balance at all. But at least we do something we believe in, right? That must be why we thank God it's Friday.

I often hear people around me complain about how they have too much work to use all their vacation time. It's a sad reality, especially since North Americans typically get much less vacation time than their counterparts in other areas of the world. My first "real" job, which was in Europe, gave me a royal twenty-six days paid time off each year, and in addition there was the option to work extra hours to generate more time off, as well as statutory holidays. My first job in Canada only allowed me fifteen vacation days, which was still better than the average ten. Regardless, I ended up thinking I was too busy to use any of it, and learned my lesson about vacation time the hard way. At every performance review I asked for more time off, but didn't end up using it. I was overwhelmed by my workload, and my perceived inability to spend time with friends and family. So my work situation both created a lot of stress in my life, and at the same time prevented me access to the remedy: getting away and taking a break. Some of my coworkers even felt that taking a leave was not encouraged in the corporate culture we worked in, despite the company's advocacy of a healthy work - life balance on the job boards. Managers viewed employees who took all their time off as less productive, and less dedicated to their work. I figured that would not be a favorable position to be in when my performance review would come around again. At one point I had multiple months of overtime and vacation time saved up. Letting me carry that much potential time off became a risk to the consulting firm I worked for. The possibility of me taking off for such an extended leave at any time wasn't feasible for them, so they revoked the excess vacation time, without warning. There was a "use it or lose it" policy in place that I clearly wasn't aware of. The company needed me in my cubicle, generating billable hours for their client. Needless to say I didn't like that idea all that much. My vacation time I had saved up wasn't something I received for free: I earned it, and worked many extra overtime hours for it. I complained to my boss, his boss, and eventually the director of the company. He got involved to make sure my earned hours were returned safely from whatever dark corner they had disappeared to. I learned my lesson, and started using my earned time off more and more, to the point where I eventually left the company.

We're living a life that's made up out of jumping through hoops that others hold up for us. And when they say "jump", we jump, often even without asking why. Too often I felt the need to escape it all, to get away and get a break from life. I don't think life is supposed to be lived that way. To me it reduced the wonderful experience of travel to something necessary to keep myself from going completely crazy. I still wanted to travel, just not use travel as an escape mechanism anymore. Instead, I wanted to use travel as an opportunity to grow, learn, and experience new things. I wanted to make travel my lifestyle, and be able to implement the freedom I experienced while traveling in my daily life. It was time for me to go explore, and see the world. In the end, we only regret the chances we didn't take, the relationships we were afraid to have, and the decisions we waited too long to make. So my new motto is to live simply, give more, expect less and love unconditionally.

For a long time I've been afraid to make the decision that I instinctively knew I had to make. As a result of my own indecisiveness I felt stuck, like a small insignificant cog in a large, supposedly well oiled corporate machine. I realized that there would never be a perfect time. If I was going to wait for the stars to align and all circumstances to be absolutely perfect - nothing would ever change. I decided to take a leap of faith, and instead of living someone else's life it was time to start living my own. With the help of several books I casted off the shackles of my existence. Not because I'm a courageous person. Like they say - courage is not the absence of fear, but the ability to overcome it. Some say life is too short to endure too many things you don't like. I don't agree. I think life is meant to be very long, and we should allow ourselves to face the possibility that we have to live with the choices we make today for a very large number of years to come. Thinking about it that way gave me an even bigger reason to change. When the day comes where my life flashes before my eyes, I want it to be worth watching. And in case I ever write them down, I want my memoirs to be interesting and worth reading.

A time and money thing

It's a time and money thing. What a great excuse to not have to do something, and blame it on something outside of our control. It's like a parking officer saying "I'm just doing my job". While that statement is absolutely true, it provides very little consolation for the fact I just got ticketed.

Many people seem to think that in order to travel as much as I do, they would have to become very rich first. "Travel is expensive", they say, and like many other things that are part of the "good life" (whatever that may be), extensive travel is reserved for the rich and famous. Being rich alone is not necessarily what I'm after. Sure, it's nice to be able to buy whatever you want - but true freedom does not come from having an endless supply of cash in my bank account. Many people that are rich are so tied up to their jobs that at the end of the day they don't have the time or even energy left to enjoy and celebrate their accomplishments. It's about having a level of freedom to live a life that I *love*. That starts with having the time to do things that I'm passionate about. A generous cash-flow does help with that, but is not always a first requirement.

It takes a bit of character to not hide behind all sorts of easy excuses, and take responsibility for your own life instead. Every single human being has a limited amount of time to spend on this planet. Some, unfortunately, have less time than others. The same could be said about money. Whether I have one dollar or one million dollars to spend, I have a limited amount of cash to spend in my limited time on earth. If I have more of the green stuff I might spend it on a bigger scale, and buy more expensive versions, of the same things. That means everyone is spending the same as everybody else, just on a different scale. For example: when I buy a house, the bank defines my mortgage budget to something that's usually anywhere between four and six times what I make annually. It doesn't matter whether I make a few thousand dollars, or a million of them every month - that just changes the scale of my budget. At the end of the day I'm still buying a house - whether I'm limited by time or money like everybody else has very little to do with it. I can be, buy or do anything I want. Just the scale changes.

"You only live once. But if you do it right, once is enough."

Mae West

I could reason there's therefore no such thing as time, or money. At the very least both are irrelevant. It's all about priorities. What do you actually want to do? Are your choices in line with your desires? What are your goals, and do you give priority to the right things to reach those goals? If something is your top priority, you'll somehow make the time, and find the money to make your goal a reality, on whatever scale you wish to be feasible and appropriate. Think about your priorities next time you decline an invitation from a friend because you have "no time". Nobody really has time anyway. It's the one thing you can't get back after you lost it. So spend your time wisely and set some priorities. Whether it's meeting friends for a coffee, looking for a new job, going on a trip, or whatever it may be you desire: do something different. Life starts at the end of your comfort zone. Take responsibility for your life, and make your choices your own. You are capable of much more than you realize.

Urgent, an urban legend

One of my former co-workers had a poster in her office that said: "A lack of planning on your part, doesn't constitute an emergency on my part." I couldn't agree more, but would like to take it to the next level: unless you're driving an ambulance or fire truck, urgent simply doesn't exist. At least not in my vocabulary. Most problems tend to resolve themselves by simply ignoring them. Or maybe they won't, but I'm taking my one risk a day, and believe they will anyway. Nothing is really that urgent, except when you see smoke, or a person in medical distress.

We're all too busy with all sorts of things that fill up our calendars. Meetings, phone calls, emails - they never end, it seems. And we all complain about it, but yet seem to get a real sense of importance out of our "busy-ness". And yet we often

> *"The problem is, you think you have time."*
>
> *Unknown*

forget what's really important, the things that matter most. The stuff that actually adds real value, and makes a difference in our own life and that of others around us. What's important is personal, and probably different for everyone. But you know what it is, for you. It is whatever it is that the voice in your heart tells you. You *know* what it is, and what isn't.

Why is everybody in such a rush in the first place? It appears everything needs to be done quickly. Just look at rush hour traffic on any given weekday. We're in a rush to get to work in the morning, and in even more of a rush to get home at the end of the day. We make quick decisions to cut corners in an attempt to shave off another split second from the commute. Let's forget about rushing, especially during rush hour. Let's stop running around pointlessly from meeting to meeting pretending to be working on something really important, arriving late and stressed everywhere we go.

Learn to breathe, relax, slow down, and get lost on purpose. There is no sign of smoke and nobody is dying.

Don't wait forever

There is something wrong with the concept of retirement. I had been consistently saving for retirement ever since my first job. Why do we put money away over a period of years upon years, just so we can live the "good life" at an old age? The world is kind of reversed that way. They say anything worth having is worth waiting for, but I'm not a very patient person by nature. Time just seems to take so much longer when I'm waiting for something. So I'll usually wait for a while, but not forever. It was early summer of 2013 where I found myself to be unhappy. I was tired, overworked, and constantly stressed. So I decided to take a mini-retirement, in my early thirties. I left full-time permanent employment, to do something for myself.

A few comedians have already pointed out how the order of life is more or less reversed, and unfair. Just as a hypothesis, I considered their proposal: In my next life I would like die first, and get that done and over with. Then I wake up in a nice retirement home, and I start to feel better every day. After a while, I get kicked out for being too healthy, so go off to collect my pension. When I eventually start work, I get a gold watch and a party on my very first day. I start with a top salary, and work for forty years or so until I'm too young to work. During the course of my career I'll earn a little less money every year, but given the

*"People wait
all week for Friday
all year for summer
all life for happiness"*

Unknown

high salary I started with that's not even a problem. After my career I get ready for high school: I party, drink alcohol, and I'm generally promiscuous. When I'm ready for primary school, I become a kid, play, and have no responsibilities. Then I become a baby, and spend my last nine months floating in luxurious spa-like conditions with central heating and room service on tap, and then... I finish off as somebody's orgasm.

So why save all the good stuff for the end? Why wait to travel until retirement? Don't wait on time to show the right decision, because time won't wait for you. Too many people are waiting for the day to come where they don't have to wait anymore. We're not getting any younger, and some people unfortunately never even make it to retirement. Others find their retirement savings don't even begin to cover the plans they had, if there's any savings left to begin with. The time to start living life to it's fullest potential, is *now*.

The benefits of taking a detour

I've traveled down a lot of paths, and, thanks to my limited sense of direction, taken my fair share of wrong turns. When I was in high school, someone told me travel wasn't "anything more but an expensive detour home". Detour or not, the benefits of travel are well worth the effort. More importantly, anyone can have access to those benefits. Travel has a positive impact on all seven areas of life: spiritual, mental, social, physical, family, career and even financial. To me, travel plays such an important role in my life that I use it as an eighth area of life to set goals for.

Travel has been proven to boost personal well-being, and improve the way the brain operates. I always feel less stressed and more refreshed when I come home, and I enjoy a better, more positive attitude towards life as a whole. Travel seems to enhance my physical and mental health, both of which are important to

> *"Two roads diverged in a wood. I took the one less traveled by, and that has made all the difference."*
>
> Robert Frost

my overall well-being. Research has shown that being able to take time off and travel can even have a positive impact on people diagnosed with (circumstantial) clinical depression and insomnia. On top of that, travel improves my personal and social life, and it even has a positive impact on home and family life. Not only does travel provide a way to grow as a person, it allows couples and families to spend quality time together and get to know each other on a deeper level than before. Travel allows us to grow a deeper bond with ourselves and significant others in our life. Life is a journey in itself, and is made by the people we travel with.

Taking a break from work to travel can even have financial benefits, despite the cost of the trip or potential temporary loss of income. If I'm feeling better overall, including my mental and physical well-being, my happiness and productivity at work will go up as a result. I might get inspired to grow in my career, or even try on something completely different. Either way there's an opportunity to become more successful in life, which in turn could lead to an increase in income over time. If everyone would start using up all their unused paid time off, that in itself would generate many new jobs for others to fill, benefiting the economy as a whole.

All of this, and more, can be had as a result of travel. I therefore consider the money I spend on travel an investment in my future. The return on my investment has the potential to generate a large return in all seven (or eight) areas of life.

Life is a permanent vacation

This parable is shared in a few different variations across the world. I'm ending this Escape section with my take on the story:

An American tourist, on a long overdue vacation, was standing at the pier of a small village on the Mexican coast, when a small boat with just one fisherman docked. Inside the small boat were several large yellowfin tuna. The tourist complimented the Mexican on the quality of his fish, and asked how long it took to catch them.

"Only a little while." the Mexican replied.

"But then, why didn't you stay out longer and catch more?" asked the American.

The Mexican explained that his small catch was more than enough to feed himself and his family. On the good days he would even give a few fish to some of his friends and neighbors.

The tourist then asked, "But what do you do with the rest of your time?"

The Mexican fisherman said, "I sleep late, fish a little, play with my children, and take siesta with my wife, Victoria. In the evening I stroll into the village where I sip wine, play guitar, and sing a few songs with my amigos. I have a full and busy life, señor."

The tourist laughed, and said, "I have an MBA from Harvard and I can help you. You should spend more time fishing; and with the proceeds you would buy a bigger boat. With the proceeds from the bigger boat you could buy several more boats. Eventually you would have a fleet of fishing boats. Instead of selling your catch to a middleman you would sell directly to the consumers; and eventually you would open your own cannery. You would control the product, processing and distribution. You could leave this small coastal fishing village and move to Mexico City, then Los Angeles and eventually New York where you could run your ever-expanding enterprise."

The Mexican fisherman asked, "But, how long will all of this take?"

The tourist replied, "Twenty, maybe twenty-five years."

"And after that?" asked the Mexican.

The tourist laughed and said, "That's when it gets really interesting. When the time is right you would sell your company stock to the public and become very rich, you would make millions."

"Millions? Really? Then what?"

The American said, "Then you would retire. Move to a small coastal fishing village where you would sleep late, fish a little, play with your kids, take siesta with your wife, stroll to the village in the evenings where you could sip wine and play your guitar with your amigos."

I now get the story.

PLAN

READY TO TURN DREAMS INTO GOALS,
AND PLANS INTO ACTION?

The value of experience

The most important thing I get out of travel is something I call *Experience Value*. Experience Value doesn't directly translate to a dollar amount. Admitted, I might have to spend a few dollars to have access to a certain experience, but there's no direct relation between the amount of money I spend on a trip and the experience value I'll take out of it. I've traveled on a very tight budget and had the time of my life. I've also experienced some of the more extravagant sides of travel, involving helicopters and limited edition limousine rides to and from "hot" party locations. Having seen both extreme ends of travel, I realized that going for the more extravagant options doesn't always make for a guaranteed good experience. Money doesn't buy happiness. If I'm not in the right mindset, or company, to enjoy and savor each moment, I'm simply not going to get the maximum potential out of the experience. So while the dollar value of that experience might be high, the return on my investment, which is the Experience Value I take out of it, is still low.

Happiness comes first. While it's a lot of fun to charter a helicopter and fly over Manhattan just to get a certain angle for a picture I had always wanted to take, those experiences have never become a mandatory requirement for me when embarking on a trip. If they were, I probably wouldn't travel anymore at all. The budget required for each and every trip would become astronomical, and prevent me from ever leaving the city I live in. When starting to plan for a trip, simply being at a certain destination is always enough for me. Going to Paris, or any other destination for that matter, doesn't require a laundry list of attractions, guided excursions and tour buses lined up to experience the city properly. The only thing that matters is getting from where I live to where I want to be, and calling it home for a little while. Soaking in

"Too many people spend money they haven't earned, to buy things they don't want, to impress people they don't like."

Will Rogers

all the energy, smells and sounds a destination has to offer. I've been to Paris a number of times while I was still in college, and all I could afford to do was roam the streets, soak in every smell and gaze at every sight I could find.

Total cost of that trip was a tank of gas (my old European car at the time was much more efficient than my current "small", per North American standards, SUV) and a couple of nights in a cheap hotel. All in all much cheaper than a night of bottle service in a Las Vegas nightclub. I applied the same principle when traveling to many other destinations. And I still use this principle today. Just being there was the experience I wanted, and all it took was to just go. The real value of *experience*, is priceless.

Breaking the piggy bank

Travel is something I consistently save money for. Ever since I first started making money, I've used the rule to "pay myself first". Out of every pay cheque I received, I would set aside a certain amount that I would only use for travel. From what was left I would pay the bills, the mortgage, rent, and so on. At times the amount was very low, as low as ten or twenty dollars, because that would be all I could afford. But regardless of the amount, the first ten dollar bill out of every pay cheque was reserved for travel. When done consistently, even small monthly or biweekly amounts add up, and have funded both small as well as larger trips.

I've taken some big financial risks in my life thus far, and in the end they have all paid off. "Take one risk a day" I read somewhere, on a plastic shopping bag if my memory serves me well. I took that advice to heart. Looking back I sometimes wonder whether certain things really where the smartest thing to do, and I can only begin to imagine how stupid some of my decisions must have looked to the outside world. So while I don't advocate gambling, especially with money, letting go of control a little bit every once in a while has been an excellent teacher for me.

It turned out most of my financial planning was very conservative, to say the least. When I met one of my financial advisors a few years ago, I arrived at that meeting by motorcycle. It was a bright and sunny day, so making the most of it by combining the financial meeting with a ride seemed like a good idea. During the meeting we discussed my risk tolerance, and as always I was leaning towards a very conservative approach to managing my finances. With my motorcycle helmet on the desk, the advisor asked me the obvious question about the mode of transportation I had selected that day. Pointing at the helmet, she commented on how many people would perceive that as taking an unacceptable high risk. It's true - statistically speaking, motorcycles are quite possibly not the safest way to get from A to B. They do not come equipped with air bags, seat belts, wrinkle zones and the laundry list of other safety features that have been implemented in cars over the years. On a motorcycle it's easy - if you get in an accident, your chances of survival are slim. My motorcycle instructor had once told me that all the protective gear we wear is mainly intended for the family, "so they have something presentable to look at for your funeral". Despite the obvious risks, I really do enjoy riding my motorcycle. I have taken numerous safety classes to learn as much about riding as possible. So while I take the risk, I do so informed: I have learned and practised several manoeuvres that have already saved my life on more than one occasion. Being able to stop, avoid or get away from danger at any point is usually a lot easier on a bike than it is when driving a car. Provided they are used correctly, there are many options to get out of tight spots on a bike. My financial advisor made me realize that taking some level of calculated risk can be a good decision, when executed correctly and at the right time. Since that conversation, I've grown out of my conservative patterns of financial planning, gradually involving a higher level of risk tolerance.

That decision has made me more aware of my financial decisions, and I revisited many I had made in the past. I reviewed every single expense I paid, and realized there was a lot of clutter. I was overinsured, had too many cable TV channels I never used, too many cell phone minutes, a land line that only telemarketers use to contact me... the list goes on. In addition to costing me money every month, all this clutter also caused me stress, either directly (the telemarketers) or indirectly (paying for cable channels I never even watched). Cutting out all the excess from that list has saved me several hundred dollars. Those savings repeat themselves every single month. Over the course of a year that adds up to a nice amount, enough to spend on something more useful, like travel.

Where in the world to go

Now where to go? You are probably thinking of that one place you've always wanted to visit but never did. Not yet, at least. For me, that place was Buenos Aires, Argentina. I've wanted to go since I was 18, and it took me a good 12 years to get over myself and just go. I finally booked a round trip plane ticket late at night after a rainy Sunday afternoon. After clicking around on various airline websites I found a good deal, booked it and went to bed right after. I still remember waking up the next morning, when my initial shock of "what have I done now" was quickly replaced by an ecstatic "I'm finally going to Buenos Aires". Over my morning coffee I started to think about everything I could see and do while I was there. I guess I had to get over myself again.

Most, if not all, people I've met have a similar destination they instinctively "have" to visit. There's always at least one unvisited "dream" destination, but sometimes the wish list is much longer. Paris, New York, Barcelona, Rio, Tokyo, just to name a few popular places. It turns out that popular destinations are based on where in the world I am, and who I'm talking to. While I lived in Europe, I've been to many Mediterranean countries like Spain, Greece, and Italy. By now, I've come to learn that most North Americans regard these places as "dream destinations". Given my proximity to all these places while I lived in Europe, it was just an easy (and cheap!) place to go while young, unemployed and still in college. To me, a more exotic destination on the bucket list has always been Mexico. For most Europeans Mexico is regarded as a more exclusive dream destination. They consider Mexico a place you'd visit on your dream honeymoon or for some special, once-in-a-lifetime trip.

At age twenty-six I decided to relocate to Canada, after which this picture changed radically. I've learned North Americans tend to visit the Mediterranean for a special occasion, or maybe they don't even visit it at all until after retirement. From this side of the Atlantic Ocean, Europe is considered to be the exclusive destination. Sometimes people even like to brag about the fact they have visited "Europe". My reply is always "that's where I'm from", which makes the bragging less interesting, at least to me. It's just another place to go, nothing more, nothing less. And I've seen most places in Europe, but nowhere near all of it. Now that I'm based in North America, Mexico seems to be the cheaper sun destination where students go to drink their face off. In a way that's what I did in Spain. It seems Mexico is my new Spain and has therefore lost some of its allure.

> *"Wherever you go, go with all your heart"*
>
> Confucius

What a different viewpoint. Moving to the other side of the Atlantic Ocean literally turned my world perspective upside down. One of the things I took from this eye opener is that every destination I perceive to be "exclusive" or "exotic" in my mind is "just another place to go" depending on which viewpoint I choose to take. The world is a huge place, but no matter where I decide to go next, it's only a plane ride (or two) away. Once I get to my destination I can live and be there as cheap or as expensive as I want. Personally, I'm now on track to set foot on every continent within the next few years. It's all just another place to go.

Travel works in all sizes

To experience travel there is no need for me to go far from home. A trip to the next town over can be just as exciting as one across the country. I like to get away at least once a month for a short trip, and traveling across the globe every few weeks is not always going to happen. While the extended trips to different continents are nice, I'm happy that the experience of travel can also be found much closer to home. Living in Western Canada, the Rocky Mountains are within short range from my home, and a few days there put me in such a different place that I often feel I've been gone for much longer. It helps me to reset my brain. When I return, I always find I'm more productive, focused and dedicated to the work I have to do. On top of that, getting away reduces stress, which in turn improves my health as well as my personal and business relationships. I come back renewed and refreshed, which means I'm much more pleasant to deal with for everyone.

That being said, I prefer a mix of trips in my own country, as well as trips further away. The learning experience and opportunity for personal growth is much more powerful when I'm further out of my comfort zone, no longer surrounded by things I'm used to: whether it's people speaking the same language, or the same kind of stores. Remove anything familiar, and the opportunities for personal growth are amplified tenfold.

Of all the places I have visited, these are some of my favorites. Some of these places have lower crime rates than New York, Las Vegas, Chicago, just to name a few, and could be a relatively safe and easy starting point to explore the world, just in case you're looking for some suggestions:

- Netherlands (Amsterdam)
- Germany (Berlin, Cologne)
- France (Paris)
- Belgium (Brussels)
- Spain (Madrid, Barcelona)
- United Kingdom (London)
- Argentina (Buenos Aires)
- Japan (Tokyo)
- China (Hong Kong)
- Italy (Rome)
- Greece (Crete, Athens)

All of my favorite destinations have one thing in common: it's possible to live very well, without spending much. And the list includes cities that appear to be expensive, like Tokyo, New York, and Paris, just to name a few. Most of these cities I know like the back of my hand, which makes it much easier to find the cheap, but excellent, places to eat and stay.

A few words of official advice

always check the travel advisories as issued by the government before I book any tickets. Any travel advice categorized as a "warning" is usually more serious than a travel "alert". If there's any current travel warnings telling me to not visit a certain place or country, I'll scratch that place from the list or at least postpone my plans for a few years, as warnings can be in effect for several years. Examples of when a warning has been issued in the past include things like an unstable government, civil war, ongoing criminal activity, or terrorist attacks. Alerts are typically issued for risks that are of a more short-term nature, such as elections, strikes, and demonstrations.

To help me understand the advisories, in particular alerts better, I often compare them to places I've already been to in the past. Travel advisories tend to list any and all potential threats, which might make travel seem more of a dangerous undertaking than it really is.

> *"We travel, some of us forever, to seek other places, other lives, other souls."*
>
> *Anais Nin*

For example, the travel alert for Amsterdam at one point listed a small risk of "unrest due to (political) demonstrations". I'm not disputing that fact necessarily, although to say Amsterdam is not safe because of the potential for demonstrations would be an exaggeration, in my opinion. As a general rule, I typically try to not get involved in any demonstrations while travelling - and if I see one in progress (a common sight in Buenos Aires, for example), I keep my distance or even take a bit of a detour if needed.

A place to sleep at night

Quite possibly the most important part of a trip is the location. After all - if location didn't matter I might as well have stayed home. By embarking on any travel, I basically admit to the fact I want to be in a different place for a while, whether it is for business or pleasure. Some "greater good" (whether it be my boss or client in case of business travel, or curiosity to some foreign culture if I'm travelling for personal reasons) got me on my way, leaving my home and everything that's comfortable and familiar behind. Since I'm exchanging one place for another, it makes sense to add some weight to that decision, and pick my "home away from home" very carefully. I devote numerous hours, spread out over sometimes multiple days or even weeks, to select a place to put my head down at night. That being said, I've tried them all: from the top bunk bed in a hostel to exclusive, by-invitation-only resorts. Picking a place to sleep is like buying real estate. My realtor says: "the three things that are most important are location, location, and location". This couldn't be more true for travel, where everything I do is based on being in a different location. I love to soak in an unknown, unfamiliar culture and surround myself with those experiences as much as possible. This means I like to stay in a place that's a good base for further exploration. In Buenos Aires I stayed in a central location from where I could explore multiple areas of the city by foot, and also had easy access to the train and subway system to be able to get away further when I wanted to. In Paris, I often stayed a bit further away from the city centre as navigating the streets of Paris or dealing with the interesting traffic patterns by car wasn't an experience I was necessarily interested in. Finding a hotel on the outskirts of the city, but within walking distance of an express subway line that would quickly get me in to the city every day, was key on this occasion.

Most larger cities have so many hotel options that looking at the entire list can be quite the overwhelming, confusing experience. Before booking anything, I try to familiarize myself with the destination as much as I can by studying maps, online reviews and a good (preferably one) travel book of my choosing. I make a list of places I would like to see, and loosely plot them on a map. I also try to figure out what the "good" and "bad" areas are - every city has certain less safe sections I'd rather avoid spending any amount of time in, or even traveling through, especially when I'm relying on public transportation. With those areas loosely mapped out, picking a location becomes a bit more manageable. Based on what mode of transportation I'm planning on using (preferably public transport, especially in larger cities - more about that later), I find a home base close to the majority of places I'd like to visit, avoiding the "bad" areas altogether. On my recent trip to Tokyo this was especially interesting as every area in Tokyo appeared to be a city on it's own. That combined with the enormous size of the entire metropolitan area we know as Tokyo (and a super early morning onward departure flight to Manila) made picking a hotel a little challenging, to say the least. Since public transit is by far the best way to get around in Tokyo, I based myself in a great hotel right overtop of the main Tokyo train station. A bit pricey, but the room had unobstructed and therefore unbeatable views of the city skyline at night, which made the extra expense well worth the investment.

I apply the same logic to beach destinations. Although I do enjoy spending time at the beach, the trip isn't complete without inhaling some of the cultural goodness a place has to offer as well. For that reason, staying on an all-inclusive resort where you're literally confined to the resort boundaries (as they're usually situated in the middle of nowhere) is something that I only enjoy for a very limited amount of time. Preferably I'd like to pick a few places I want to visit, which in addition to old city centers and hidden churches always includes a

> *"I dislike feeling at home when I am abroad."*
>
> George Bernard Shaw

number of different beaches as well. I then find a place to sleep right in the center of it all. I do value ocean view, so the more beach front the property is, the better. Based on that wish list, sleeping in a hut built right above the salty water in the Philippines was a priceless experience. To me, there's nothing like falling asleep and waking up to the sound of real crashing waves. A sound machine with pre-recorded ocean sounds just doesn't provide the same experience. On my first ever trip to Hawaii, I picked a home base in the quieter Kihei, on the beautiful island Maui. I enjoyed exploring the rest of the island from there in a rental car. And yes, I went all out on the rental car and drove a convertible since it was my first time there - and a great addition to the Experience Value of the overall trip. Since I enjoy cooking and don't mind the experience of grocery shopping in a somewhat unfamiliar store (not sure how unfamiliar Safeway really can get, but still), I stayed in a low-rise beach front condo building. The unit I rented had a private balcony to enjoy breakfast, lunch, dinner and the ocean waves. The beach was only a few steps away; there wasn't even a road in between the building and the sandy beach. Expensive?

Not at all, especially when compared to other hotels and resorts on the island - if you do the math and calculate the cost per person per night it turned out I've paid more for a hostel bed at times. It takes a bit of research up front, but it definitely pays off both in terms of money as well as Experience Value - every time.

Ten countries in ten days

Trips and vacations never seem quite long enough. When booking a trip, it seems hard to find even a few days in the calendar to be able to get away. When the time comes to return home, it never seemed long enough. Let's look at the bare minimum. No matter how many stopovers and destinations I manage to squeeze into one single itinerary, I really need the time to settle down in every place. The day of arrival I'll generally feel lost, I'll hate the hotel (no matter how nice, exclusive and fancy it is), and want to go home. It's what I call my day-zero-homesickness. Something I've eventually learned to live with after many miles of travel. Just accepting this as one of my quirks or character "flaws", proved to be the best remedy. On the arrival day I now simply wander around town a bit, find something good to eat with a nice glass of wine (or two). Post-dinner I might do some more wandering around, after which an early night usually is in order. The next morning my entire world is different, and my day-zero-homesickness has been replaced by a sense of excitement and I can't wait to hit the streets again. My short explorations the night before now come in useful by providing a place to start for the next few days.

Knowing this, building an itinerary that allows for roughly one full day per city is generally not a good idea as it doesn't leave any time for me to get adjusted to my new surroundings. Even if I didn't suffer from my day-zero-homesickness I doubt whether one day will ever be enough to say I've actually *been* somewhere. How much time does one need to pick up on the rhythm of the destination and start to live a little like the locals do? At the very least I'll need two full days to get the most important things off my travel to-do list (more about that later). Those two days do not include travel days on arrival and departure, so this will bring my personal bare minimum number of days per destination to at least four. Even that will not allow for a lot of time, but I'm quite the slave driver while traveling and will maximize my Experience Value every waking minute. I simply have to see and soak up as much as I can. I'm up early and go to bed late, usually being on my feet all day long.

I'll use this rule of "bare minimum" when I try to squeeze in many different destinations into one itinerary. Especially if I haven't been to a certain corner of the world just yet, I find this is a great way to familiar-ize myself with as many places as possible in a short amount of time. On my recent trip to Asia I got to see Tokyo, Hong Kong, Singapore, Manila and various Philippine islands in just about a single month. For the longest time in my life I had no intention to even visit Asia. I didn't have any particular reason to not go there, it just didn't make it to the top of my list. Ending up there anyway completely changed my perspective. I've loved every second of being immersed in an entirely different culture with unfamiliar smells, habits, languages, currencies and many more things to get (at least a little) used to. On this particular trip I didn't always follow my four-day-rule, which turned out to have an exhausting effect on me. But every cloud has a silver lining. Being able to see so many places in such little time was exhausting, but did wake up the travel bug in me more than ever - I eventually returned home with a list of places I definitely want to re-visit and spend more time in.

On the other end of the spectrum, I spent an entire two-week period staying in one single place in Buenos Aires. Many people have asked me since why I didn't travel around Argentina more. I definitely was, and still am, interested to see much more of this amazing country, however on my first trip there I really wanted to soak in the culture, and get to know the city more instead of being constantly bussed around. I wasn't bored for even a split second. While I stayed in the city, there was something new to see and explore every single day. And on top of that there was plenty of time to re-visit a handful of my favorite hangout spots at night. Looking back, it feels like I actually lived there for a few weeks. That's exactly what I'm after when I'm traveling - I want to live and act like the locals do as much as possible, instead of being on the move constantly. Having the time to actually soak in the energy of a destination is something that's very high on my priority list. I know many people visit Europe with a jam-packed itinerary, and "see" over ten countries in an equal amount of days, or less. Looking at their pictures, most seem to be taken at the airport or through the dusty window of some tour bus. The luxury of being born in Europe made visiting one place at a time for a longer period a little more feasible than for those who have to cross the Atlantic Ocean first, but despite the amount of travel needed to get there, spending a week in Rome in a small studio and shopping for fresh food at the local farmers market still sounds more appealing to me than squeezing one too many places into an already full itinerary. Like they say: when in Rome, do as the Romans do.

BOOK

HOW DO YOU CLAIM WHAT'S YOURS?

The joy of booking travel

To me booking travel, especially when it comes to air transportation, is as almost much fun and comes with an equal number of complications as filing a tax return. Although I do have a few favorites, none of the many travel sites out there seem to get it right by creating a completely user-friendly, end-to-end experience that actually makes it easy and fun to book a trip. Somewhere in the process the wheels come off and the entire train derails. I've had to deal with a lot of different issues ranging from booking sites failing halfway in the booking process but still taking money from my credit card, all the way to having a confirmed seat on a transatlantic flight that was bought and paid for, but somehow no ticket was issued to me. Now try to explain that to a customer service agent on the phone; or, even more important, try to get it resolved.

If done right however, the payoff of finding and booking travel is well worth the invested effort. The biggest problem to me is the vast amount of options available: for most destinations I can pick from countless airlines and routes to get there. Combine that with the amount of options when it comes to accommodations and it's a guaranteed recipe for disaster, or at the very least a stressful experience. That's not the way a trip or vacation should start. Planning and booking a trip should be part of the entire rewarding experience of travel. This section of the book will provide you with some helpful tips and insights to master the art of booking travel, and bringing the joy of it all back into the equation.

Cutting out the middle man

We all have to start somewhere. My very first trip that involved any sort of cross-border traffic "had" to be a package deal. How else can you travel safe? Unexperienced as I was at the time, I insisted that a tour operator *must* have the best prices and options available. As with most assumptions, this one turned out to be partially true. If you're traveling anywhere popular (what the popular places are varies depending where in the world you are, as explained earlier), tour operators sometimes offer excellent value for money. They simply have the buying power to fill up entire planes and hotels at a time, and are therefore in a position to negotiate great deals with the various accommodation and other travel providers. The airfare deals I've been able to get on flights to all sorts of Mediterranean destinations (from Amsterdam) were at the time simply unbeatable compared to booking direct with the airline. But times have changed.

As part of the package experience, after arrival a transfer bus would bring me to my hotel, resort or apartment. In my case the accommodations I tend to pick usually turn out to be last on the list of the shuttle bus driver. As a result I've ended up spending an hour or even more in a transfer bus that was a little too crowded at times. I quickly started replacing the "free" transfer with a rental car so I could drive myself, get there faster, arrive more relaxed and ultimately enjoy more beach time to sleep off the minor jet lag. Without realizing it, I had embarked on a journey to become my own "tour operator", and plan more and more on my own.

The model of selecting my own mode of transportation and ignoring things that came included with the package deal I wasn't interested in, worked fine until I realized some (not all) tour operators squeeze the absolute best possible rates out of hotel and property owners. "You won't find them any lower, guaranteed!" This model does make it hard for property owners to make money. So to win back some of their margins hoteliers overbook their properties by one or more nights. It turns out to be cheaper to put guests in another hotel for a night or two than to give up their own rooms at the "lowest ever" rate to the tour operator. In the end, they too have to make money, one way or another. It's some good food for thought. While I'm all for saving my hard earned cash where possible, I don't enjoy the hassle of finding myself overbooked again and again after a very early morning departure of some charter flight, and having to phone the travel agent (on roaming charges) to complain. Basically you're somewhat homeless in a foreign country with too much luggage to carry around. After being homeless like that on two occasions I decided I had my fair share of that particular travel experience. There had to be a better and easier way.

One solution that worked well was to opt for higher-end resorts and hotels, preferably the ones that are part of a respectable, well-known chain. They have a name to uphold and usually wouldn't send me away as easily, although it did happen at times. Any property related to a chain usually works well and makes for a more reliable and predictable travel experience. Before departing I pretty much know where I'll end up, since for some chains the rooms in Sao Paolo almost look like identical copies to those in midtown Manhattan. Depending on where I'm going, this might work very well and provide a safe, predictable place to sleep. The downside is that by using chains I risk losing out on the great experiences that are to be had by staying in a

"I travel not to go anywhere, but to go. I travel for travel's sake. The great affair is to move."

Robert Louis Stevenson

local, independent boutique hotel. It's a bit more risky, as some are not as "boutique" as their well designed website suggests, but I learned that if I do my research, the bad ones can be easily avoided. As a general rule I'm always weary of websites that look a little too well designed. Some of the nicer boutique hotels I stayed at had a horrible, outdated website where the rate and availability inquiry had to happen via email, or even phone (or fax, but I personally don't have a fax machine anymore).

For me, a better alternative to using large booking sites is to deal with the hotel directly, and cutting out the tour operator as the proverbial middle man. Sure, that might mean I miss out on some of the package deals, but I haven't found myself overbooked at any hotel or resort since, and the room I received was almost always upgraded to a higher class. One time I got bumped from a standard "economy" room to a split-level suite with a real wood burning fireplace without even having to ask for it, or paying a dollar more. Now that's the type of "overbooking" I like: getting the best room of the house simply because it's empty and no one else booked it. My experiment worked - good hoteliers all over the world seem to appreciate their individual guests just a little bit more than the block of rooms that is secured and paid for through a large operator. It's a simple principle. If I imagine myself a hotelier - anyone that comes in on the very lowest rate possible where

I'm hardly making any money probably ends up in that weird space behind the elevator that I managed to convert into a room somehow. The guest that booked on my very own (outdated!) website I'll at least accommodate in the room of their choosing, maybe even something better if I have it available.

From my perspective as an individual traveler - if any hotel sends me away, I'll make sure to never, ever set foot on that property again. If they send a few tour operator guests away, there's a fresh bus load coming again in a few days. As long as not too many people complain to the tour operator and they uphold some acceptable level of service that will probably be the case for years to come. It does take a bit of effort to find these "good hoteliers", though. Reviews in travel books and magazines are great, but for those places mentioned in popular travel guides rates tend to be on the higher side as these places usually are (or have become) extremely popular. Travel websites have reviews on even the smallest motel far-far away, and are an excellent way to separate the good from the bad.

Once I have selected a couple of options, I'll have to be my own tour operator and do some budgeting to see what the total "package" will cost me. In my budgeting I include airfare when needed, as well as other transportation, because transfers to and from the airport are usually not included if I book everything by myself. That being said, some hotels and resorts provide a complimentary airport transfer or can at least assist in arranging one when asked. When it comes to accommodation, I've learned I can usually book directly with the hotel at the same nightly rate as offered by the tour operator. This is due to the fact that "advertised prices" or "rack rates" aren't necessarily the price the operator pays to the hotel, which can be much lower. In other words, the hotelier doesn't like seeing his own booking agents "undercutting" his own price so doesn't allow them to actually advertise the lower cost. So if I can source the accommodation at the same price as what I would have paid to the tour operator, all I have left to do is find a way to get there. If air transportation is needed I might get lucky and find a good fare directly through the airline - which in my experience also reduces the risk of being overbooked, especially if you hold a frequent flyer card for that airline (more about that later). With the many low-cost airlines operating in Europe finding a cheap fare is easy. In other parts of the world, especially North America, it can be a bit pricier to jet around in which case selecting a packaged option might be a cost effective solution. Consider all your options and pick the one that works best.

I believe I can fly

Over the years I've learned to break the process of booking travel down in manageable, bite-size pieces. I start with a rough esti-mate for a timeline: when do I want to travel, and for how long. The less precise at this point, the better. For me it usually comes down to any given quarter in a year where I want to plan a trip, for typically anywhere between three to six weeks at a time. After setting a rough timeline, I try to familiarize myself with the available options for accom-modations and their price-range in the period I want to travel. Just some basic, general information is enough at this point. Nothing is set in stone yet, and usually my plans and time period do tend to change a bit when I learn more about where I'm going and what options are available within a certain price range, as prices do tend to fluctuate throughout the year. While accommodation is an important part of the travel experience and thus the booking process, the most cost savings are to be had by getting there in the first place: airfare. My personal rule is to always fly for free, as I'll explain in the next chapter. Trying to find an affordable fare does limit the days on which I can travel. Flying for free typically imposes even more restrictions when it comes to flexibility of the days I want to arrive and leave. But even when, on occasion, I decide to pay for a ticket (with actual money), getting to the destination is key. I do not always wait for the absolute lowest fare available. Paying less than average is not only good enough, but also a personal requirement when booking anything. I won't settle for paying above average price, because in most cases there's no need to. Most traditional airlines end up with a plane full of people who all paid a different price for their seat. Some of the people on board got their seat for dirt-cheap, others paid top dollar. For the same seat that is, I'm not talking about the difference between economy and business class, or even the preferred comfort seats with less tight, "extended" legroom. There are some, but very few exceptions to this rule, so when I board any aircraft, I'd like to be in the group of people that paid less than average for that particular flight.

I book my tickets either a few months in advance, or last-minute. It depends on the type of trip I'm taking. For some international travel booking too last-minute takes away some of the fun, as well as the ability to appropriately plan for the trip. This becomes important especially when I'm not familiar with the destination just yet. Doing research and booking accommodations both take time. Then again, planning too far ahead can become costly if my travel plans or circumstances change. Quick getaways, like a few days in Las Vegas or New York, I'll often book less than a week in advance.

There are a few tricks to get on board with the "below average" group. Flexibility in travel dates is common knowledge these days - as long as I can avoid the vacation and holiday rush, I'll have the best odds to save significantly on airfare. I usually get the best deals by planning my departure and return between Tuesday and Thursday. Other days tend to be popular with people taking an extended long weekend, and are therefore more expensive. In addition, the day on which I make the reservation itself appears to make a significant difference as well. You can certainly use that rule to your advantage, even if you're, for whatever reason, bound to travel in school vacation periods. Most travellers book their vacation when the entire family is at home: weekends and evenings. The airlines take advantage of this by inflating their ticket prices during peak "booking" times. Usually, I'll end up paying (much) more for the same ticket booked on a Sunday afternoon compared to booking that ticket half an hour past midnight on a Tuesday or Wednesday night later that same week. It's almost like the stock market: prices go up and down, and there are graphs to be found online that show historical pricing for airlines and destinations. I research those religiously and use them to my benefit. There are even online services available that will monitor airfare, and send alerts by email or text message of any changes. I'm prepared to act quickly if I see a fare that interests me - it can go up again in a matter of hours, and might not come back down. While there certainly is a pattern to the prices that repeats roughly every week or month, the highest and lowest point on that cycle can fluctuate significantly.

In addition to monitoring the average fares, special promotions and seat sales can also be a great way to secure a cheaper seat. I'm careful with my wording here: *promotions* sometimes mean the airline is simply "promoting" the route, without necessarily lowering the fare, so those don't always get me a better deal. Seat sales on the other hand often bring significant savings, however taxes and additional fees aren't always included in the advertised price. Either way, the sales and promotions especially come in handy when I'm flexible as to where I'm going. Some larger airports will even sell off "no show" or cancelled tickets: I can take a seat of someone who didn't check in for their flight on time, or cancelled it last-minute. These are hard to come by, and until I get to the airport I'll typically have no idea what the destination is going to be - so packing is a little tricky. If I'm up for the adventure this is a great way to travel, but it requires the ultimate flexibility: other than the departure day (more or less) I'll have little idea where I'm going and for how long. I might end up on a beach for five days, or in a winter wonderland for an entire week. Regular seat sales are not as aggressively priced, but as long as I can be somewhat flexible when it comes to travel dates (they're usually offered in the low-season around spring or fall) as well as destination (the airline might not offer a sale on a destination of my exact choice, so I might have to be flexible and opt for another beach instead). Again, being ready to act quickly and not trying to pay the absolute bottom price is key. I once lost out on a very cheap transatlantic flight to Amsterdam since I thought the fare would drop further. It didn't. I waited too long, and ended up paying just about double the price that was offered during the sale, for the same seat. I definitely learned my lesson the hard way on that one.

Instead of booking all flights at once, it sometimes is advantageous to break the entire itinerary into smaller pieces, especially when I'm traveling for a longer period of time through different destinations. The multi-city or multi-destination tickets offered by major airlines aren't always the most affordable, so I'd rather fly to an international hub and book one or more separate tickets with a cheap local airline. Especially in Europe and Asia there are many small price fighters that will sell seats for cheap. I've often traveled between Paris, Rome and London for less than a hundred dollars, including all taxes and fees.

Once all the flights are booked, I go back to my list of accommodations and simply fill in the blanks for the rest of the trip, one baby step at a time. Since there are usually less airplanes landing at the destination on any given day compared to the amount of hotels available, this should be relatively easy. I pick a place to sleep that I like based on price as well as reviews or my own past experiences. With a flight and hotel secured, it's time for me to start thinking about what I want to do while I'm there.

The Freedom Project

I believe I can fly for free

The biggest hurdle in traveling is to actually get to the destination. I'm forced to spend hours in an air-pressured cabin to get to where I want to be. For that reason alone some people choose to not travel at all, simply because they either hate or are too afraid of the experience of flying. Whoever said that it's not about the destination but about the journey probably either likes flying a lot or has never seen the inside of an actual airplane. "The goal justifies the means", seems more appropriate when it comes to boarding economy class airplanes. Personally, I don't mind flying. It's a great way to physically remove myself from everyday life on this planet. Seeing the world, with all its problems and worries, reduced to ant-sized creatures, puts things in a great perspective somehow. This is why I still appreciate the simple pleasure of having a cup of coffee at 30,000 feet (as well as those airlines who pride themselves in serving decent coffee). If you have a low caffeine tolerance and are planning to get some sleep on your next overnight flight, you might want to pass on the coffee as well as the alcoholic refreshments, since caffeine, alcohol and medication are typically doubled in strength thanks to the altitude and air pressure. That applies to sleeping pills, too. In my case, coffee soothes me so I'll sleep better after a hot cup of Joe. I guess I enjoy the simple things in life, especially when those simple things are offered to me high up in the sky, in a seat I got for practically free.

After spending most of my life savings in exploring this planet, and spending the rest of it on a transatlantic move to Canada, I thought

I was done traveling for a while. That idea didn't really appeal to me. There's so much more out there to see. One of the reasons for moving to Canada was to explore North America more. Doing that from a North American base seemed like a good idea at the time. With little savings left after the move, I was determined to crack the "code" and fly for free, or at least really cheap. The good news is, that it's actually possible to get on board of a plane and pay nothing or next to nothing for the ticket. It's been just about 5 years since I last paid for an airline ticket, and in that time period I've been able to travel all over North America, South America and Asia. And I even managed to squeeze a trip to the homeland in there, which adds Europe to my list of continents I've traveled to in just the last couple of years only. The concept I apply to fly for free is generally referred to as "travel hacking", but that makes it sound much more complicated than it actually is. I tried to follow the principles of travel hacking for a while, and found it took a lot of time and effort, with very limited results. Maybe I just wasn't dedicated enough or too lazy to really make it work. Anyway, my method is simpler, easier, and best of all: it can be followed by anyone. It doesn't cost anything to get started, and if I can do it anyone can.

The secret is in travel rewards cards: credit and charge cards that give me travel points for every single dollar I spend on them. When I first learned about this I signed up for every program that's out there. I gained some points, but nothing really happened - I was a long way away from getting any actual "reward". Sure, I could get some nice gadgets for my points and miles, but not the actual travel I was after. The key, as with many things in life, lies in focus and dedication. I researched the amount of points or miles required for long haul as well as short haul flights, and selected only a few programs that provided the most value for my points. I'm simply not interested in those programs where I need 50,000 points for a one-way flight just to get across to another city in North America. If I'm lucky enough to get one point for every dollar spent that means I would need to spend 100,000 dollars to get a "free" return flight. I might as well just buy the ticket at that rate - and sometimes that is indeed the best option. I ended up selecting only two programs to participate in - one that provides me with easy access to short-haul flight to the next city, province or state, but doesn't score very well on long-haul flights. For the long-haul flights across North America, or even to Europe, I picked another rewards program. I now fly across North America to New York for about 25,000 points round trip. I can get a return ticket to Hawaii for about 45,000 points. Since I accumulate one point for every individual dollar I spend on my charge card, I need to spend approximately 25,000 dollars to get a free ticket. Since I charge everything, literally everything to my card, that's actually relatively easy to do. Groceries, dinners, clothing, presents, cups of coffee, regular bills, business expenses, everything goes on my card. If I spend anywhere between 1500 and 3000 dollars a month I'll typically fly for free at least once a year. The more regular expenses I'm able to charge to my card, the faster I can travel. Since I charge things I have to pay for anyway, like my cellphone bill, to the same card, that amount is not limited to spendable income only - which brings flying for free within reach for pretty much anyone. The question no longer is *if* I will be able to travel, it's just a matter of *when* I'll get there (and where I'll decide to go next).

In addition to regular points there are bonuses to be had, starting with a nice welcome bonus when I sign up. Sometimes these are upwards of 30,000 miles, which, on the right program, gets me a free long-haul flight right away. If I choose a rewards program that's partnered with the credit card provider, I can accumulate miles on top of the credit card company points as well and "double dip". For example paying for gas at the right gas station gets me both miles from the gas station, as well as points via the card I use to pay for the gas. When I first heard about these "travel hacking" methods I thought it was a little shady, but it's all perfectly legal, and it works. Using this

> *"To travel is to discover that everyone is wrong about other countries."*
>
> Aldous Huxley

approach actually allowed me to fly for free to Buenos Aires, Hawaii, Las Vegas and Vancouver in less than one year. I don't spend that much and lost most of my points on the Argentina ticket, but thanks to a special promotion I wasn't even aware of I got most of them back as a bonus before I even returned from that trip.

I do want to include a word of caution. While I do use credit cards to pay for anything and everything, I don't ever carry a balance. I strictly use my cards as charge cards and pay them off at least every month, but usually every two weeks. While credit card companies are great at providing me with free travel, they also charge hefty interest rates when I do carry a balance beyond the initial "grace" period (usually a fixed number of days, anywhere between two to four weeks). The interest rates on outstanding balances can be significant, and potentially about a third of the entire balance. Paying those rates would completely defeat the purpose of being able to fly for "free". This is why I've never paid a penny in credit card interest, and the card providers love me all the same for it. Most recently my favorite provider actually offered to pay (with my points) for a hotel I had stayed at. I thanked them but declined as I strictly use my points for flights only. Hotels or other means of accommodation are simply too easy to come by: once I get to the destination I can make the trip as cheap (or expensive) as I wish by carefully selecting my places to sleep and eat.

Another thing to mention is the taxes on air travel. Unfortunately those usually cannot be paid for with points on most airlines. I haven't found one that does, however some credit card companies will now offer to pay for the entire bill by means of a "purchase eraser" program - I make the purchase and have them pay for it afterwards with points. It turns out that paying for the taxes with points significantly increases the amount of points needed for a trip, which is why I tend to just pay the fees and taxes. I've never paid more than approximately 150 dollars in taxes and airport fees on my "free" airfare, and that was on a long-haul return ticket to South America.

I've also learned a good way to accelerate my earning of points and miles is to gradually upgrade to higher levels of premium credit cards, one step at a time every six to twelve months. I start with the most basic (often a free) card, and then work my way through the ranks. Every time I upgrade I usually get a nice upgrade bonus, as well as a higher earning ratio so I'll accumulate miles and points even faster. Keep in mind there are typically annual fees to be paid at the higher levels. This is another reason to stick with one (or maybe two) programs, and really focus on those. I'm pretty extreme in being consistent (putting my OCD tendencies to good use, as I'd like to call it), and will go to a different retailer or supplier if my premium card of choice is not being accepted. I tell them politely they ruined my next vacation by not allowing me to earn my points, followed by an executive summary of this book, and me leaving the store. I also made sure my own company accepts pretty much any type of card as I'd like to give my clients the choice to use their preferred card, even when I started out very small.

If I can do it, you can too.

Become an insider

There's no need to own everything we use. Sometimes having *access* to a certain experience is enough. For example, if my neighbor had that fancy convertible sports car that I've always wanted to drive, and he likes me enough that he lets me have the second key to use the car whenever I want, there's no real need for me anymore to spend money to buy that sports car myself. I already have access to it, with presumably no strings attached. Being an insider, and having the key, is what matters.

While traveling, being an insider and having certain cards and memberships are what can make all the difference. It gives me access to experiences that enhance my travel experience, like business class lounges, even when I fly economy. And it protects me, to some degree, from bad experiences, such as being bumped from a flight because I got overbooked. I hate the concept of overbooking with a passion. Pretty much every airline does it these days, but I think it is daylight theft and should be outlawed. How can anyone think it's good customer service, let alone morally acceptable, to sell a certain number of seats, or rooms, more than once? We're not talking about time-sharing an airplane seat here. It's an outrage, in my humble opinion. Luckily there are a few things I can do that offer some degree of protection against this kind of corporate greediness, and I consider it my moral imperative to share them with you. Contrary to how I handle rewards programs (I only use a select few), when it comes to frequent flyer cards I have them all, and then some. Come to think of it, I might even have duplicates for some programs. While I do earn some form of miles or points on most of them, they usually expire well before I'll ever reach a sufficient level to convert them into a reward ticket. I don't mind that, as I already get my free travel rewards from the selected programs I focus on. The reason I still carry all these frequent flyer cards with me is that, in my personal experience, airlines seem to overbook their "frequent" guests less often. After being left behind in the airport by a major European airline, I felt pretty blue and vouched I would never let them do that to me again, ever. Even though airlines won't confirm (or deny) this, being part of their frequent flyer program seems to make enough of a difference in their love for me to not be left behind anymore. In addition, having a confirmed seat number right away when I book the ticket, as well as checking-in for the flight online the minute check-in becomes available, helps in getting bumped from the flight altogether.

Sadly enough, some airlines feel the need to charge for anything and everything, including selecting a seat during the booking process. As long as the fee isn't too outrageous, I usually accept it for convenience sake (albeit under loud protest at my computer screen). The other advantage of early online check-in is that I might get myself a cheap upgrade to business class. I once flew business class on a transatlantic flight I had paid for entirely with miles. The upgrade to business class only cost me 300 dollars one-way. I checked in online the minute the flight became available for check-in, which in this case was twenty-four hours before departure. I didn't have to think twice when the offer was presented to me. The gentleman that ended up in the seat beside me had paid well over ten times that amount for his ticket. I hope somehow he gets a copy of this book.

A second place to call home

While it doesn't relate to booking travel directly, indirectly owning or not-owning a timeshare or second home does have an impact on the need for additional accommodation and booking habits, so I want to touch on the subject here. Buying a timeshare seems like an affordable way to obtain a second home, or at least part of it. For the rest of my life I would need to book less accommodations after this one investment, according to the sales pitch. I've been approached by sales people trying to sell me a timeshare on the premise of this assumption in quite a few places. Most activity seems to be around beach and ski destinations. Of course Las Vegas is a popular one too. The sales pitch is simple, but effective: don't we all say we want to go on vacations more? Now if I go on only one trip per year, the timeshare will basically pay for itself in only a few years. Following their well thought out marketing materials the math definitely works out. If I were interested to go on vacations to exactly the same place year after year, I would have considered the opportunity to buy a timeshare more seriously a long time ago. Unfortunately for the timeshare sales staff I like to stay flexible, and cover as much of the planet as possible. That usually doesn't work with a fixed timeshare location. Maybe I'm different than most, and get bored too easily. I like having my roots at home, but while I'm traveling I like to be free and unattached. I love each and every place I have visited so far, and would love to go back and revisit quite a few of them, but to keep coming back to the same place over and over again is not something that appeals to me. Even when I do go back to visit the same destination again, I usually like to stay in a different area or neighborhood to get to know the city better.

When it comes to timeshares, I've also experienced that some of these come with certain restrictions to keep the property manageable for whoever operates it. Because of that most timeshares don't come with a lot of flexibility. When planning a trip to Las Vegas one particular timeshare, that I might have been able to enjoy, only allowed arrivals and departures on Friday or Monday. Being the popular North American weekend destination that Vegas is, these days of the week turn out to be the most expensive to fly. So in the end it was actually cheaper to pay for a hotel and flight package arriving on a Tuesday than it would have been to fly in on Monday in that same week and enjoy the "free"

> *"We wander for distraction, but we travel for fulfillment."*
>
> Hilaire Billoc

timeshare accommodation. It makes the sales pitch from the timeshare staff less attractive. Even if I wanted to go on a Vegas trip every year, the investment would most likely pay off over time, assuming I'm willing to pay extra for airfare since I can only arrive on certain dates. So while I'm definitely no expert when it comes to real estate and the novel concept of time-sharing a property it does seem to limit my flexibility when traveling in one way or another, so I'm still not interested.

Living close to the Rocky Mountains I know quite a few people who have a second home or cabin somewhere in the mountains, some of which are timeshares, others are fully owned. Admitted - having a cabin in the mountains seems a very ideal and romantic lifestyle addition. From my perspective it also proves to be quite the attachment. The countless hours spent driving the same roads between home and the cabin is something I would get bored with in a while as well. In addition cabins need lots of maintenance too, sometimes even more than the often newer home inside the city limits. While the idea of owning a mountainside escape definitely appeals to me, the responsibility that comes with it is not something that fits well with my current lifestyle or way of traveling. I'd much rather head out to the mountains, which I do at least once every month, and rent a different cabin or condo in a different town each time. I have fewer responsibilities that way, and get to experience a bigger variety of places to visit. But like I said, maybe I just get bored (too) easily.

PREPARE

IS THERE A PURPOSE
TO BE PACKED AND READY TO GO?

A note to self

Often I write myself notes to remind me of all the things I have to do in a certain day. I live by the virtue of to-do lists. They help me stay organized, and get things done.

I'm also a big believer in learning by experience, and I've learned almost all of what I share in this book the hard way. A prime example is packing my bags, and getting ready to go. Saying I'll travel light this time, and actually doing so, are two entirely different things. Maneuvering two heavy suitcases, my camera equipment and backpack through Tokyo station after a long eleven hour flight, wasn't pleasant. Especially since I wasn't familiar with the station. I found out only after arriving there, that this station consists of a multi-level underground city. I really wished I had taken less stuff with me. I vouched right there and then, tired and angry at myself in the middle of Tokyo station, to write a "note to self" telling me to pack less and travel light, and leaving it in my suitcase for next time. That note turned into this section of the book instead.

One man's trash

Watching TV is not something I do very often. But when I do, I enjoy watching those shows where people bring in old things they've always had in their basement, and it turns out to be something of great value. My grandfather took this idea to heart, and collected furniture that other people were getting rid of. He would store it in his house for future use, just in case. One man's trash, is another man's treasure. Humans are "pack rats": we tend to collect an abundance of things that might come in handy one day. You don't even have to be diagnosed as a hoarder. Everyone has things hidden in a closet or basement that they don't particularly need, now or ever. For a while my basement had a collection of duplicate, old furniture that I was planning to either sell or give away for free to someone who might need it more than me. That never happened. Instead more and more accumulated in my basement, and every item itself accumulated more and more layers of dust. If I truly wanted to live a more simple life, I decided I needed to get rid of all the clutter. I donated anything that was in good shape to charity, and paid a garbage removal service serious cash to have the remainder of the mess removed. When I saw their bill I knew one man's trash truly is another man's treasure. At least I freed up some empty space, both in basement and my wallet.

I inherited some of my grandfathers habits, and had a hard time getting rid of certain things, especially the ones that had some sort of memory or sentimental value attached to them. I really had to get over myself. If I couldn't deal with loosing an item I'd try to sell it on a classified ads site. Especially gadgets and electronics seem to do pretty well. That way I converted some of my clutter into cash, which I could use while traveling. I've funded a number of smaller trips this way, by just converting clutter into cash.

I've moved to different homes, cities and even a different country more than I cared for in my life. I don't particularly hate moving, as to me it's a great way to declutter my life and tidy everything up, and then start from

> *"Simplicity is the ultimate sophistication."*
>
> Leonardo da Vinci

scratch somewhere else. When packing for a move, I follow a strict rule to make sure I'm not bringing too much: for every box I pack, I have to fill up at least one garbage bag with things I'm throwing out, giving away to friends and family or donating to charity. When unpacking the boxes in the new home I often question why I decided to bring certain things anyway, and end up tossing almost a quarter to half of what I brought with me. This process has shown me the eighty-twenty rule applies even to worldly possessions: it's the twenty percent of the things I own, that I use about eighty percent of the time. The remaining *eighty* percent of my possessions is a waste of space and money.

And the same eighty-twenty rule applies when traveling. For many years I carried too many things with me that I barely even needed, if at all, while abroad. The one advice most experienced travellers will give when asked, is to travel as light as possible. Get rid of all the unnecessary clutter.

Credit card, camera and passport

Packing is one of the most daunting tasks while leaving for a trip. I almost always leave it to the very last day, which does create some unnecessary stress. It also forces me to think quickly, and travel light. I've found that regardless the length of the trip, I have a tendency, like most other people, to over pack and bring too many clothes I hardly wear, or wear at all. They simply come with me, stay in my suitcase, and smell a lot less fresh by the time I make it back home. So when I come home again I end up putting clothes I didn't even wear once into the laundry - just to make sure they'll be nice and fresh for the next trip. It took me quite some time to understand what a waste this is. More importantly, I realized that the length of the trip doesn't affect the amount of clothes I'll really need. Even on longer trips, I enjoy wearing the same comfortable clothes over and over again. I know they have enough pockets and zippers to carry the things with me I'll need during the day. They dry quickly in case anything gets wet by rain, or my unbreakable habit to get too close to any body of water I'll encounter. To address my over-packing, one time I wrote a note to myself after I came home, and put it in my suitcase so I would find it the next time I had to pack for a trip. The note included the amount of clothes I had actually worn on the last trip (about half of what I packed) and underneath, in capitals, "travel light". I laughed when I found it the next time, a few months later. It prompted me to embark on a little experiment and travel extremely light that time, bringing hardly anything at all. It was a short trip of just a few days to a different city, so I figured the risk was manageable. To my surprise I didn't miss or forget a single thing.

Over the years, I've created a collection of clothes that I only wear while traveling. So now, when I leave for a trip, I just move that set into my suitcase and call it a day. If it's a longer trip I'm fine with finding a laundromat somewhere to clean my clothes, or have the hotel clean them for me. Having the hotel do laundry can get a little pricey depending on where I'm staying, but with some hotels my clothes looked better than when I bought them new, complete with individual boxes for each piece of clothing. If I completely run out or find I really need something I didn't bring with me, I'll just buy it at the destination. That way I'll have to buy local and at the same time get to know the destination a little more. Buying practical things like soap and toiletries really helps to get to know a city, and you also prevent the bottles from exploding in your suitcase. By shopping local I also end up with some practical souvenirs - even if a shirt doesn't have the city or country name printed all over it, to me it still is a memory I take with me from that trip.

"If you wish to travel far and fast, travel light. Take off all your envies, jealousies, unforgiveness, selfishness and fears."

Cesare Pavese

Today, most of the clothes I wear are bought on one trip or another. Traveling and packing this way even turns out to be cheaper than wasting money on tacky souvenirs I'll never look at again. By the time I get home those souvenirs almost always have lost the allure they had in the souvenir shops. Something practical to me will always carry the memories and Experience Value of the trip, regardless of whether it's recognizable as an obvious souvenir to someone else or not. After all I don't need to prove to anyone I've been to a particular place on the world by wearing the city name.

If I took my travel light principles to the extreme, the things I'd really need while away from home are my passport (makes getting in and out of most countries a lot easier), and my credit card (so I can buy anything I forget or need). Being a photographer, taking my camera kit with me is also an essential. Technically it could be replaced, but I love my camera and set of lenses and accessories I have for it. Replacing those would take a good chunk of time out of my travel schedule. For me, that list of only *three* items should cover it. Anything I bring in addition to that is a benefit which makes my life potentially a bit easier - however it shouldn't be too much. Finding an exploded shampoo bottle on arrival definitely doesn't make things much easier, or enjoyable.

So, in conclusion, here's what I typically bring on any trip:
- One week of clothing, including one semi-formal outfit
- Passport
- Camera
- Credit cards
- Copies of all travel documentation

Really, that's it.

The little things add up

Flying has changed tremendously over the last ten years or so. When I first got introduced to the wonderful world of air transportation, which is not that long ago, things were pretty friendly. A kind word or genuine smile would easily get an overweight suitcase past the scale and on board of the plane, without paying any extra fees. On one particular occasion the next guy in line who was less friendly to the check in staff had to pay to get his bag in. His bag was in fact nowhere near as heavy as mine, and we were both boarding the same transatlantic flight from a very busy and crowded New York airport. I like to believe smiling did make a difference and made the experience pleasant for everyone involved.

It does seem that mentality has changed. Or maybe my smile has faded to something beyond recognizable, but nowadays I'm having issues getting any sort of luggage on board without paying, regardless of whether it's overweight or not. It appears that most airlines have adopted a model where I pay for even my first bag that is well within their weight and size restrictions. Personally, I'm not overly happy about this. How am I supposed to travel if I can't even take things with me anymore without paying the airline again? Let's not forget this is after already having obtained a (sometimes expensive) ticket, either with my points or actual money. A lot of people appear to silently agree with me on this topic, and as a result everyone is reverting back to hauling as much stuff as humanly possible with them into the aircraft cabin. From my layman's perspective this does appear to slow down the boarding process quite a bit. It's been well over a year (if not more) since any of my flights departed on time, give or take five minutes. Most flights I take nowadays are delayed by at least 15-30 minutes compared to the scheduled push back time. My guess is the time it takes to get the cabin organized with all this added carry-on luggage might have something to do with it at the very least. You can imagine my surprise when on a recent flight carry-on luggage was taken at the departure gate, and checked in "free of charge". After paying some twenty-five dollars earlier at the check-in counter to get my small suitcase checked in on that trip, I wasn't overly excited about this process. After that experience I'm now one of those people who travels even lighter, and hauls everything possible into the cabin as carry-on.

Despite the savings on luggage fees this has brought me, I did learn the hard way that juggling my cameras, carry-on bags and a tray of food in the airport restaurant requires some serious balancing skills. Skills that I don't necessarily seem to master, especially when I'm attempting to enjoy my travel experience. Experience Value also counts right at the airport, after all. Given the amount of stuff I pay for on my airline ticket (fuel surcharge, noise reduction fees, etc.) I'm not too excited when I have to swipe my credit card again to simply get my belongings that I more or less need on my trip, from A to B. I already paid for the ticket, and in my humble opinion bringing some luggage when you're traveling for more then a few nights is just common sense.

Common sense unfortunately isn't always that common anymore. The amount of stuff I pay for on a ticket is overwhelming - it varies from "fuel surcharges" to "noise cancellation fees" because some city planner decided to build an airport right next to a densely populated area, or vice versa. After a while they forgot whether the chicken came first, or the egg. More and more companies are copying the ideas airline executives have put in place. Things like a "fuel surcharge" keep popping up more frequently. Recently I noticed a courier service dared to charge me a fuel surcharge for delivering a letter within the same city. If you can't beat them, join them - so for a while I tried adopting the airline model by charging my corporate clients for a "fuel surcharge" myself. They all laughed at me, as they should have. Of course I forced no one to pay but I thought it was a fun experiment. I wish we would all laugh some more when something happens that we don't agree with. I, albeit politely, protest every

> *"Once a year, go someplace you've never been before."*
>
> *Dalai Lama*

time an airline makes me pay for a first checked-in bag that's within the normal weight and size limits. To not upset anyone waiting in line behind me I usually don't make a big deal out of it, and simply pay the fee. I do mention I'm not too happy about being charged. If more people were to politely, and calmly, state when they're unhappy about something, it might eventually lead to change. I'm not always this positive though. When one check in agent was about to charge me a hundred dollar for a bag that was less than a pound over the limit, I was about to repack and hold up the line for as long as needed. Luckily the good man came to his senses and "waived" the fee (thanks, again).

Personally I try to be aware of any and all fees, if possible. While airlines never fail to surprise me with new "surprise" fees and charges, awareness does help. So does a simple luggage scale that I now take with me everywhere I travel. The twenty dollar investment paid off on the first trip. As I tend to buy at least a thing or two while traveling, my suitcase is well below the weight restrictions when I leave home, but almost always overweight on the way back. While there was a time I just smiled and paid the fee if needed, now I like to avoid them by balancing the weight between my carry-on and check-in before heading for the airport. This has already saved me hundreds of dollars in the past year only, simply by weighing my bags myself before I arrive at the airport. No one really wants to re-adjust their packed underwear in front of a busy check in counter, so doing it while I'm still at the hotel and making adjustments when needed is a much more comfortable and pleasant experience. Another thing I keep in mind every time I travel is that overweight fees are typically higher than fees charged for a second bag. So as a backup plan, I take an empty, folded bag with me in my suitcase that I can fill up if needed on the journey home. Checking in a second bag allows me to take much more with me, for typically a lower fee.

No guarantee of future results

The foreign exchange market is the largest market in the world. Brokers want to make me believe that serious money can be made by buying and selling foreign currencies. No other market has the same volume of transactions. The major players on this market are the larger international banks, who have enough buying power to turn small changes in price movements, into large profits. When I asked my financial advisor if there was a way for me to get in on the action and do a little investing myself, I was warned that past performance is no guarantee for future results. So there's risk involved, I get it. That also applies when traveling, albeit on a smaller scale. Truth be told, I haven't found a successful and efficient way to deal with the problems created by the need to carry foreign currency just yet. It's easy enough to simply take out cash from some ATM, but I always end up overpaying on fees, and if I'm not careful I end up taking out too much money which literally will have lost it's value by the time I return home, so I just end up spending it all on things I don't need anyway. I do have a couple of tips and ideas I'd like to share. Bear in mind I'm not an economist. Then again, as I've mentioned before, travel is the only thing you can buy that can make you richer, and my aim therefore is never to travel as cheap as possible, even when I'm on a budget. But wasting hard earned dollars unnecessarily on useless things like exchange rates and bank fees doesn't seem to be a lot of fun. My tips are therefore focused on avoiding waste where I can.

The only one that seems to truly benefit from exchanging money back and forth is the bank: why else would there be a different exchange rate for taking foreign currency out versus bringing it back at the end of the vacation? Not surprisingly, the difference between the buying and selling rate of foreign currency is in the bank's best interest, not mine. This is why, when I do end up with too much cash on hand, I'd rather spend it all and not bring any foreign currency back home with me, unless I'm going back to the same place in the very near future. "Spend it all" to me means the limited amount of cash that I had on hand when I landed. I always like to have some local currency on me the minute I land, which makes tipping taxi drivers and hotel porters, or just buying a much-needed bottle of water, a lot easier. Landing with the equivalent of one or two hundred dollars usually does the trick for me, and on most trips I don't get any additional cash, as I charge everything I can to my credit card, just like I do at home. This prevents me from having to carry around lots of cash, and more importantly it earns me points and miles towards my next trip. I literally fund my travel with travel, like perpetual motion. Carrying some cash however is inevitable as not every country is setup to accept credit cards. To my surprise I found Japan

> *"The main purpose of the stock market is to make fools of as many men as possible. "*
>
> *Bernard Baruch*

to be a hit and miss when it comes to paying for food with plastic. For such a technologically advanced country I expected the opposite. A few extra trips to the ATM got me the cash I needed and it all worked out just fine.

To prevent me from having to figure out bank account balances while traveling I prefer to take a cash advance on my charge card instead of using my debit card. Fees for this service vary and can be rather high, so I make sure I'm aware of the costs every time before I leave, as they do happen to change from time to time. I also contact all my card providers before I leave to make sure they are aware of my travel plans. Without that "travel note" on my account foreign transactions often get flagged as fraudulent and are therefore declined, which can be a bit of a hassle to get resolved - especially when I'm trying to pay for a rental car just after arrival in a different time zone late at night. Most debit cards work fine too as long as the bank is part of one of the large international networks. I just look at the logos on the back of the card and compare those with the ones on the ATM machine. The bank also takes a, sometimes hefty, transaction fee for each cash withdrawal, so to avoid losing too much money on transaction fees I plan ahead and take enough cash out for a couple of days, usually another one or two hundred dollar equivalent each time. I don't like carrying more than that around to prevent getting mugged. I've gotten lost in less favorable areas of New York on more than one occasion. While I've always found my way home unharmed and with all my possessions on me, at those times I'm extremely happy to not have too much cash or other valuables on me.

When things don't go as planned

Despite planning ahead and being aware of my surroundings sometimes things do go differently than planned, for better or worse. In the movie "The Terminal" a passenger arrives in New York to find out his country technically didn't exist anymore after he arrived due to political complications, rendering his passport null and void. Usually the immigration officer at the border will send back anyone arriving without the required paperwork, however in this case there technically was no country to send the passenger back to, leaving him in the weird land that belongs to nobody: the airport arrivals and departure lounge.

While traveling there are many things that can go wrong, hopefully nothing as significant as finding out your passport is reduced to a piece of meaningless paper. There is a broad spectrum of insurance products available that will take on part, or all of the risk when things go wrong. However, a lot of trouble can be avoided if I know where to go beforehand. Where do I go to ask for anything that I might need in case of potential trouble? Whether or not I carry additional health insurance while traveling, I still need to know how to obtain the required medical assistance should I, or anyone in my group, need it. Having the insurance policy in itself doesn't necessarily make a difference, obtaining the right care does. A lot of health care policies, especially the ones that provide additional travel coverage, will have an emergency number that gives access to assistance when needed. A similar service can be obtained from most major credit companies, ranging from emergency assistance, to helping me secure a place to sleep or eat, or even getting emergency cash in a local currency if all else fails. I've never had to use any of their services (not even the restaurant reservation service as I like to figure things out on my own), however having assistance available just a phone call away gives me much needed peace of mind. Especially when traveling solo, like I did very often, it's good to have some form of backup. Knowing what number to dial, and *how* to dial it when needed, is key. I always program emergency assistance numbers into my phone and keep a paper copy with me as well, since smart phones are a popular item to get stolen in most parts of the world. Family and friends back home prove to be less useful if anything bad happens, because they're more emotionally involved than an emergency assistance operator. In addition they might have to do extensive research to figure out how to get access to cash, medical assistance or a replacement passport or bankcard. Most emergency assistance services deal with things like that daily, and are able to resolve a lot of things relatively quickly.

GO THERE

HOW DO YOU BRIDGE THE DISTANCE
AND FEEL CONNECTED?

One step at a time

Nothing matters more to me while traveling than the experiences I gain on the way. It's those experiences that turn into the memories and stories I take home and carry with me the rest of my life. In this context, the saying "it's not the destination that matters, it's the journey" is very applicable. Every step I take on my journey should be a valuable experience. It applies to everything, from the smallest insignificant detail like a meal or a cup of coffee, to the main purpose that made me decide to embark on the journey in the first place: it should all be something worth remembering.

To me, a trip begins the second I lock the front door of my home behind me and get in the taxi to the airport. To me, "travel days" aren't a necessary evil to simply get to wherever I might be going. While leaving my home behind always stresses me out a little as I want to make sure everything is in perfect order for when I return, the second I close that door behind me my trip has officially begun. I'm enjoying the ride to the airport as if it were a cleansing process in which the mundane, everyday life gets washed off of me. It's a process where my mind and body prepare to soak in the experiences that await me. Like a sponge my mind cleans itself from all the tension I accumulated, ready to soak up new and fresh experiences. Even though getting through the airport might be a bit of a hassle: getting my boarding pass, the luggage checked in, making it through security and immigration - they are all baby steps that are part of my journey. Every time I complete one of those steps I regard them as a small victory that's worthy of a little celebration. I quickly forget the pesky unexpected overweight baggage fees, security inspections, immigration formalities and their associated long lineups. Once all of those are behind me and I've made it to the peace and quiet of either an airport lounge or a coffee shop, I typically find I'm at ease, relaxed, and ready to embark on my new adventure. To mark the moment and celebrate the new beginning I'll treat myself to a nice meal, snack and a glass of wine (or cup of coffee, depending on the time of day). A new adventure awaits me.

Life itself is all about taking baby steps. Dream big, but think small, and take one day at a time. That applies even more so when traveling. It's all about these *small victories*; one thing, one challenge, one lineup at a time. This way I'm breaking the entire adventure of travel into small, manageable bits. Turning a month of trekking through Asia into baby steps at a time makes it sound a whole lot better to me. Without the baby steps the entire trip might start to sound like an insurmountable journey. With that mindset I might have ended up staying home, on the couch, which sounds a lot easier to do. But breaking a big undertaking down in bite-size chunks can make the hassle of travel a lot easier to deal with. That process starts while I'm at the airport, getting ready to leave. And the victories continue, especially after the plane has landed. Getting my luggage back on the other side of the world is always a great moment, especially if it rolls off the belt in the same one piece as I checked it in. Then, finding ground transportation and eventually making it to the place I'll be staying at for the next little while are all huge things that are often neglected. I make a point out of marking those moments. I savor them, and I'm proud of myself for making it that far already. It turns a "travel day" full of mandatory hassle into an enjoyable feast that's part of the trip. Managing to deal with practicalities such as getting around, whether by taxi, public transit or otherwise, getting a cup of coffee, finding something to eat, are all huge accomplishments, especially when I'm in a foreign country, unfamiliar or even hostile territory that I've come to love and appreciate over the duration of the trip - one baby step at a time.

It starts at the airport

Airports can be a tricky place to navigate, and everyone gets a little stressed by just the thought of all the hassle that comes with it. My vacation mindset starts to kick in the second I get to the airport or even on the way there, but it gets really going after I'm done dealing with the check-in, security and immigration checkpoints. To get to that vacation mindset sooner rather than later I'm one of those people who arrive at the airport extremely early. I've arrived well before the check-in crew on more than one occasion. Admitted, being that early might not be the best use of time. Still, getting to the airport early avoids stress, and long check-in lineups. Before leaving for the airport I try to check-in online whenever I can, since that way I can pick my seat myself. Also, the sooner I hold a boarding pass the less my chances are of being bumped to "overbooked" status. To secure my favorite seat (usually over the wing on the far left or far right of the airplane to mitigate the effects of turbulence as much as possible), I make sure to check-in online the second it becomes available. Checking in online doesn't always work, especially when I'm traveling to a destination that includes one or more transfers or stopovers. It appears online check-in systems are just not smart enough to handle those more complicated bookings (that sometimes even make the most seasoned check in agent frown). In those cases I'd rather check-in at the airport, where I also have the chance to ensure my bags will go all the way to the final destination by themselves, without the need of me picking them up somewhere in between. Sometimes I do have to pick up my bags and clear them through customs on a stopover destination myself, which greatly increases the amount of time needed on a stopover. I make sure I know when booking the flight how much time I need for stopovers and transfers - and plan my time accordingly.

Depending on the airport I'm flying through, security can be more or less of a hassle. Most of the officers on duty are pretty friendly these days, but I have encountered exceptions. I treat them like any other government official: with the same respect I'd like to be treated with myself. I've never had any serious issues getting through. The same applies to immigration, although traveling through North America on a European passport while living in the Great White North isn't always easy. On occasion I find myself answering more than the usual amount of immigration questions. I have nothing to hide, and since I'm about to spend my travel budget in the country the

> *"It is better to travel well than to arrive at the right destination."*
>
> Robert Louis Stevenson

immigration officer is representing they always welcome me in eventually. The recent improvements with pre-screening programs have greatly enhanced my experience, and I found officers I dealt with after enrolling in such programs almost friendly. While I'm no expert when it comes to the important topic of national security, one of the things that seem important to them is whether I'm actually a tourist or (illegal) immigrant. By default everyone appears to be placed in the latter category. As long as I can make it clear I'm a tourist, which means I'm planning to return home at some point, I never encountered many issues. A return airline ticket is usually accepted as solid proof of my intention to return to my home country. So in addition to my passport

I always come equipped with printed copies of my itinerary and any other documented travel plans I have.

After the whole check-in, security and immigration dance is completed my vacation truly has begun. If I have a long time to wait I'll try to get into the business lounge, which provides a much quieter experience than the "regular" departure lounges. I usually get in on one of my credit cards, or one of the other membership passes I hold. But even if I don't, some lounges offer a "day-use" fee for stays up to a couple of hours. Depending on the food and drinks that are included with the fee, it's usually worth it especially given the much quieter atmosphere. Some even offer showers, which on long layovers between flights are very refreshing. It's all about the Experience Value. Why wait enjoying the travel experience until I get to the destination?

Punctuality.

Airline punctuality is a sensitive subject to me. I find it stressful to know that I can be denied boarding when I arrive at the departure gate only minutes late. Luckily this has never happened to me since I'm always extremely early, but the thought itself of being left behind in a departure lounge doesn't make me happy. It's just not a pleasant idea to have my vacation mindset come to such an abrupt and unexpected end.

My biggest frustration is that especially since when I do arrive on time, it seems perfectly acceptable that the airplane hasn't even arrived yet when boarding time comes around, and passengers end up waiting up to thirty, sometimes even sixty or more, minutes past the boarding time, with no or very little announcements being made. I understand delays do occur and are inevitable at times, but more and more delay time is accumulated due to things like the "late arrival of the inbound aircraft". It suggests airlines have optimized their turn around times to a point where even the slightest variation in the process could be the cause of a serious delay.

Punctuality is a bit of a double standard, and waiting is not my favorite pastime. While I personally think it's important to voice your opinion in a polite manner at all times, there's usually very little that can be done but to be on time and wait, more or less patiently.

Dinner and a movie

There used to be a time when food and drinks on board of an airplane were included. It's been a bit of an adjustment to get used to bringing my own picnic lunch on board, especially now liquids don't make it past security checkpoints anymore in most airports. Even the cabin crew of one of the airlines I was a frequent flyer on at the time, protested when they first heard about the fact they weren't serving food anymore. Initially the crew was afraid they would get bored as they would have nothing to do. That wasn't true, at all. They were supposed to provide the same service as before, the only difference being they now had to charge passengers for it. Most of the crew was fine with that idea, at least it gave them something to do. The thing about change is that we'll eventually get used to anything. Time heals all wounds, they say. I don't agree. We just learn to deal with it, accept it and eventually move on.

Paying for food is one thing, but having to pay for the onboard entertainment system is another, and not something I enjoy doing either. To my surprise some airlines recently required me to swipe my credit card to activate the TV in the seat in front of me. Until I did, the screen kept blinking in big letters "activate now and watch ... ". If I close my eyes I still see the blinking words. The entire entertainment selection on this flight consisted of two movies, that weren't all that recent in the first place. I took two flights on one particular airline: a five-hour one to get to Houston, and a short connecting flight to New Orleans. On the one hour I could bear the blinking "activate now" when dimming the screen as much as possible. On the five-hour leg of the flight it was too annoying, so I swiped my card and watched the old movie.

Most airlines have a pretty good selection of movies, and especially in the newer model airplanes the screens keep getting bigger and bigger. I was most impressed with the "wide" screen display that filled almost the entire headrest in front of me when I flew to Japan. The system came with a great selection of shows and movies, too. It just makes the time go by a little faster, especially on long-haul flights. After my New Orleans experience I now check with the airline before departure to see what kind of TV system they have. If it's anything I have to pay for I try to load some movies or TV-series onto my tablet. It's a lot cheaper than paying for a poorly stocked in-flight entertainment system, and I know beforehand I'll have something to watch I'll enjoy. And as an added bonus there's no interruptions on my tablet for bi- or even tri-lingual announcements about the weather or in-flight service.

When it comes to fees and charges, including those for entertainment, awareness makes all the difference. It allows me to make an informed decision about what I'm doing instead of just swiping the card and paying the surprise fee. I'll provide my own dinner if I have to, and will bring a movie too.

Forget about the jet lag

There are many jet lag tips available. Everybody goes by something different. After many transatlantic flights I have tried the majority of the so-called remedies. None of them really work for me, so you might as well skip the rest of this chapter. Flying is exhausting for most people, because our human bodies are not necessarily designed to spend long periods of time in an air-compressed tin can 30,000 feet above the ground, while being packed in seats that barely give enough room to breathe, let alone stretch. Also, in particular after 9/11, "congregating" in the aisles makes the airline staff nervous and for most airlines it's even against the airline's security policy. So we're told to relax, sit back, and enjoy the flight. It seems there aren't many other options available than to sit back, anyway. Since I don't sleep very well (if at all) in an airplane seat, I usually spend my time catching up on some movies on the in-flight entertainment system or my own tablet. I try to enjoy myself, relax as much as possible in a confined space, and just accept the fact I'm going to be pretty tired and sore by the time I get to where I'm going. It's all part of the experience. Killing time with some of the anti-jetlag exercises in my seat is fun too, especially when combined with the occasional stroll to the lavatory. Why not go on a little field trip and use the one in the back of the plane? The ones in front are almost always reserved for business class, so unless I'm seated in that part of the cabin I find I get in trouble by crossing the "magical" curtain that separates business class from the rest of the world.

What worked best for me in dealing with jet lags has more to do with a mindset, than with little exercises. First of all I had to accept the fact that a body that isn't used to the more or less hostile, or at least unfamiliar, environment of an airplane, will be tired as a result of having to deal with that environment for any extended period of time. After boarding many long-haul flights, I started to get less tired. I took nine hour flights every other month, and my body slowly got used to the experience. I follow a few simple steps every time I travel, that all boil down to adjusting to the time zone of my destination the minute the airplane door closes. That means I'll adjust my watch to the new time zone *before* the plane even takes off. I'll start adjusting my time on board of the plane to that of the new schedule. I find that even if I don't change anything else, my mind gets used to the new time quicker when I see it on my watch (or phone, in flight mode of course) hours in advance. I'll try to get into the rhythm of the destination as soon as I can by eating and sleeping on the new schedule right from departure, instead of after arrival. Even though I don't sleep well on a plane, just closing my eyes for a while helps me relax, and with any luck I might even doze off for a few minutes. Drinking plenty of water on board of the plane helps to stay hydrated and counteract the fatigue, and dry air, as much as possible.

After arrival, I'll carry on with my day as if I had been there for weeks already. I eat and sleep as the locals do right away, even if I'm exhausted from a red-eye overnight flight. Only if I really need to, I'll take a half hour nap, but will set an alarm and get out of bed when the thirty minutes are up. If I can I'll skip the nap as it usually makes me feel worse anyway. I try to stay awake until the new local bedtime, or at least 9pm. Following this routine my body gets rid of the jet lag within the first twenty-four hours after arrival, instead of battling it for a week or more if I give in and allow myself to sleep when I arrive. Having a good meal on arrival helps too. When crossing the Atlantic Ocean whenever I go to London (UK) a traditional English breakfast on arrival always gives me an extra boost. I typically don't enjoy a heavy breakfast, but it sure works wonders to combat the jet lag symptoms.

That's all I do. A jet lag is caused by the difference in time zone, so the only thing that works is to bridge that gap in time sooner rather than later. The sooner I start adjusting to it, the sooner I'll be up and running after arrival. What better way to use the time spent in an aircraft to start counteracting the jet lag so I'm ready to go once I get there? That way I start arriving before I even take off.

How to get upgraded

Somehow I never seem to get the room or accommodation I've booked. Which is a good thing: I always end up in something nicer than what I had reserved. I've been asked many times how I do it. The answer is very simple: I just ask. By traveling at less busy times, most hotels have lots of available rooms when I arrive and they often don't mind bumping me up to a higher class simply because I ask politely if they have "something nice" available. I'm specific in my request, as asking for an "upgrade" is a great trigger for the person on the other side of the counter to bring out a price list for available upgrade options. Instead I ask directly for what I want, and I'm either very subtle with my request by asking for "something nice" in general, or more specific "something nice with a view". I don't always get upgraded to a full suite, but more often than not I get something nicer than what I've paid for. Sometimes I forget to ask and discover the room is not to my liking when I open the door. It can be either too noisy, or have a horrible view of an opposing wall. Whenever that happens I simply return to the check-in desk without touching anything, and ask if they have anything better available. One exception aside, where the hotel in a small mountain town was truly fully booked for a wedding, I've always gotten a better room as a result of a polite, subtle request. The one exception just proved the rule to me. I'll also never go back there.

This idea of just asking, politely, for what you want, even works when flying. Especially on long-haul flights, I always go up to the podium in the departure lounge and ask if there are any upgrades available. I've been able to secure a business class seat for just about a hundred dollars (on a free ticket) a few times, which then also gets me additional (free) luggage allowance, access to priority boarding and free food and drinks in the business class lounges. When timed right, it can be more expensive to not upgrade the ticket than to pay a little extra and enjoy the experience. If the flight isn't too crowded, some airlines will just give an empty business class seat to anyone who simply asks. It never hurts to ask for what you want, you just might get it.

Shuttle or limo?

In addition to flying direct whenever I can, there's a lot more ways to ensure I get to my destination as wrinkle free as possible. While group shuttle services at most airports provide a very cost effective way to get to the hotel or accommodation, I've certainly not found them to be the most efficient mode of transportation time-wise. I ended up waiting in a shuttle or taxi line-up one too many times, wasting valuable travel minutes in the airport even after I technically already had arrived at my destination. There's no bigger waste of time. And time is the only commodity we cannot get more of. A minute wasted I'll never regain. Making a point out of not wasting precious time is at least ten times more important while I'm traveling. So instead of cramming myself into uncomfortable shuttle buses, waiting for other late passengers with their luggage piled up mile-high beside me, I often choose the comfort of a private transfer instead. There are plenty of options, depending on where I'm traveling to. For example, in Las Vegas, my preferred and only mode of transportation is a stretch limo. In most cases they're cheaper than taking a taxi, especially if I'm traveling with three or four people who wouldn't have fitted in one taxi anyway. On other destinations, I've even skipped the "free" included transfer bus in exchange for a rental car or private transfer. I'll always get there faster, and definitely more relaxed. And speaking of Experi-

> *"It is better to see something once than to hear about it a thousand times"*
>
> *Asian Proverb*

ence Value, taking a stretch limo into the city can be quite the experience by itself. When I get to the hotel, I arrive relaxed, and in style. I'm ready for what else the day might bring me. All of a sudden a boring transfer that's part of the already written-off "travel day" becomes a fun experience on the first day of vacation.

Early and late check-ins and outs

Part of the hospitality industry is to be a good host and accommodate to the needs of the guest. I understand that juggling a lot of rooms and creating a smooth check-in and check-out experience can be a tricky job for reception staff at hotels. But then again, that's their job - not mine. When I arrive at a hotel a little before their official check-in time, I'm very appreciative if they are able to let me into my room, instead of into a storage facility for my luggage. It's just good service, and something the hotel can plan for if I give them my estimated arrival time and flight details when booking the room. There's nothing more annoying when arriving at a hotel after a long flight to find out they're strict about their check-in time when all I want to do is fresh up and maybe take a short nap. I've been sent back onto the streets at 1.30pm when check-in is "not until 2pm" after a long bumpy flight to Hong Kong. I didn't make a big deal out of it and just went to get some lunch. When I'm visiting Hong Kong next time I'll probably pick a different hotel.

The same goes for checking out. It does seem that most hotels charge extra for late check-outs, while an early check-in is usually free, if provided at all. Being a member of the hotel chain's free preferred guest program usually comes with a few simple benefits including complimentary early check-ins as well as late check-outs. Either way I don't like to pay for arriving early or staying late, unless it would create a really big inconvenience for me. Spending an entire day on a Spanish beach resort waiting for the 7pm transfer bus on a day where it just wouldn't stop raining was anything but pleasant, and in hindsight I should have just paid for the late check-out on that occasion. Similar to the early check-in, a late check-out was no option in the hotel I stayed at in Hong Kong, but with a relatively short onward flight to the next destination in Asia later that afternoon I was planning on using my last few hours there by exploring a few more places before leaving anyway. So I just put my bags in storage and hit the streets one more time.

BE THERE

HOW DO YOU LIVE YOUR TRAVELING LIFE
AND FEEL MORE ALIVE?

The first meal

The traveling lifestyle is all about getting in the right mindset. This doesn't happen right away. First of all it requires me to simply enjoy myself. Being in a state of joy is what matters. Letting go of all cares and worries, and focusing on doing those things that bring me joy. Skiing, hiking, swimming, or being less active and just sitting on the beach. It will put my mind at ease, and allow the creative juices to flow freely. This doesn't happen right away, but usually after a few days I notice I start to feel refreshed and new ideas and inspiration start bubbling to the surface of my subconscious mind. When that happens, it's not something that takes any effort at all - it's the letting go that's the hard part. Being in different surroundings does help a lot with the process of letting go, and not thinking about anything.

What I wrote earlier about Experience Value doesn't stop after dealing with the airport - that's just the beginning. I use my time at the airport to get into the right mindset right from the start, and then continue to seek out more experiences throughout the trip. I'm not necessarily talking about extreme experiences like bungee jumping or skydiving. I'm talking about celebrating and marking every moment. For example having a nice ice cream or glass of wine to celebrate the moment of first arriving at the destination. It doesn't have to take much, or be expensive at all. The point is to savor all of those moments, as those are the experiences I'll be taking home with me.

Following that same principle, I don't like to have a quick meal on arrival at the first restaurant that catches my eye. The food usually turns out to be disappointing and the service even worse. Being stuck in a bad tourist-trap restaurant is such a waste of a first evening in a new and exciting town. Instead, I like to take the time to enjoy a really nice meal. It doesn't matter whether it's a four-course event at a fancy place, or a hole-in-the-wall take-out. I'm determined to find something that I'll enjoy, and fits the occasion. With the multitude of review books, sites and even (offline) smart phone applications available it's pretty easy to find something within walking distance on the fly no matter in which corner of the world I'm staying.

My travel to-do list

What to do while traveling greatly depends on the type of destination. Obviously a beach destination will inspire me to do and see different things than a city trip to New York. Still, my approach to deciding what to do, regardless of the destination, is roughly the same. While I'm one of those people who actually loves to spend time on the beach, I do prefer to select a beach destination that has a colorful cultural offering within reach as well. This allows me to go explore to my heart's desire, and then rest up and catch some rays on the beach. What I'm interested in doing the rest of the day depends on whether the place I'm visiting is brand new to me, or if I've been there before. If it's a new place, I pick and choose a few things from any top-ten list in a travel guide book. To me it's a great way to start exploring unknown territory. It helps me to find the popular tourist spots and get them off my list quickly. I'll also mix in some non-top-ten places that appeal to me, or were suggested by friends as a "must see" before I left. When that's all done I just wander off the beaten path, and end up finding the greatest little hole-in-the-wall shops and eateries.

If, on the other hand, I'm going back to a place I've been to before I usually don't re-visit many touristy places I've already seen. Although I love the Eiffel Tower, I've only made the climb to the top once or twice, as I don't enjoy the long line-ups that go hand-in-hand with world-famous tourist spots. Besides, the Eiffel Tower can be seen from most corners in Paris as long as I'm somewhat elevated. Most rooftops or anything with a view will do. By seeing the famous Eiffel Tower from different angles I'm creating a different experience every time.

In the end, deciding on what to do all comes down to a mix of research, and suggestions by friends as well as locals. If I can, I'll start my research early while putting together the itinerary and booking the trip. Other times I didn't even open a travel book until I was already in the plane headed for my new home away from home.

> *"Certainly, travel is more than the seeing of sights; it is a change that goes on, deep and permanent, in the ideas of living."*
>
> *Mary Ritter Beard*

Leaving things to the very last minute can lead to great results, and on this particular trip I simply jotted down a laundry list of places to see and neighborhoods to visit. I create such a list every time I travel, whether it's weeks before or on the plane ride there. It gives me some peace of mind that I'll see the things that are most important to me. I don't want to miss out on seeing something unique I was so close to, but only learned about when I was back home on the other side of the planet. I don't use the list to plan out every minute of every day; it's just a list of possible places to see. If I make it to about eighty percent of the places listed I consider myself a happy camper, or traveler. It's always good to have a few things left to see so I have a reason to come back another time.

While traveling I truly live by the day. I'll decide on where to go next the night before, or even the day of at breakfast. Once I pick the main attraction for the day I'll quickly run down my list to see if there's anything else close by that day. For efficiency's sake I might as well try to see anything in the same area on the same day, if time permits. This way I'll quickly put together a day jam-packed with activities and places to see, but still leaving enough room to explore the area around the main attraction. I've found some of my favorite shops, coffee bars and restaurants this way, offering a more authentic travel experience, literally minutes away from the tourist crowds. Those are the ones I go back to on subsequent trips. Having a curious mind and a sense of adventure really does pay off while traveling.

We are what we eat

Food is often, in addition to transportation and hotel accommodations, regarded as the biggest contributor to overall cost of the trip. Common sense tells us it must be really expensive to eat in large metropolitan cities like New York and Tokyo, just to name a few. I decided to test this out and traveled to New York, for the first time in my life, on a very tight budget. I was working my way through college at the time, which should say enough about the amount of money I had to spend: virtually nothing. I spent my entire savings account on a pre-packaged hotel and flight deal, which at the time worked out well for me. All I had left for pocket money on the trip was the contents of my piggy bank. Those pennies had to last about a week and buy me meals in a city that's considered one of the most expensive in the world.

Since New York, and North America in general were both completely new to me (I hadn't traveled much beyond my home town at this point in my life) many things I'm now familiar with were something I really enjoyed at the time (and still do, actually). For me, *being* in New York was all that really mattered. My first breakfast in the city that never sleeps was a croissant and coffee from a stall on the street corner. I saw people pick up their coffees and breakfast pastries from there on their way to work, so I acted like the locals do and lined up to get my share of the street corner goodness. Admitted, street food always smells better than it tastes, but nonetheless I enjoyed the experience and huge cup of coffee that I got out of the deal. That was followed by a large coffee from the hotel take-out bar the next morning, and on the third day I "treated" myself to a sit down breakfast in a small diner tucked away in some side street I saw the night before. Again, I found myself surrounded by locals who quickly stopped in for a bagel on their way to work. That diner was my first bottomless coffee experience in my life, one I'll never forget simply because I wasn't used to the novel concept of free refills. Total cost for my "expensive" treat-myself breakfast was well under ten dollars.

Most lunches and dinners on that particular trip were equally cost-efficient. As a European resident I wasn't very familiar with another North American concept: food courts. I really enjoyed the cheap but decent food, together with locals on their way home after a long day in their skyscraper offices. I did enjoy a few "sit-down" dinners, however most of those were in relatively cheap Italian restaurants a block or two away from the busy main streets. By avoiding the main streets most of the time when I was looking for food I found some fantastic meals, for a very affordable price.

I learned that to find good, or at least decent food, I sometimes have to go off the beaten tourist path a bit, and maybe adjust my expectations when needed. All that really mattered to me was to be in a place so far away from home, and take in the sites and some of the attractions I wanted to see. This model of traveling became one my first "best travel practices" for my future journeys. Being there is what really matters, and as long as I managed to stay well fed, not go hungry or starve I was doing great. The *art* of traveling to a place completely foreign to me, and managing to get something to eat and drink, even when I don't completely understand the language, or don't have a lot of money to spend, is one of those small victories I still enjoy every time while traveling.

In later trips, my budget was based on a corporate expense account and therefore not as strict as before. I learned it can also be a lot of fun to enjoy a good food experience in some of the finer restaurants. It would be a shame to miss the unique eating opportunities that a lot of destinations have to offer. It's all about finding the right balance. On subsequent trips to the Big Apple I've enjoyed some great meals outdoors on the long summer nights in Battery Park, watching the sun set over the Statue of Liberty. Needless to say this was a bit of a different experience than my beloved food courts, which comes with a different price tag. It was well worth it. On the other nights I still ended up going back to the cheaper places that I remembered from my first trip. In the end, my expense reports were claimed to be well *below* the average for the company, despite the many nice things I treated myself to.

To tip or not to tip

Tipping has become a bit of a controversial topic for me. I've worked in the "service" industry for many years, and nobody ever left me a tip. Consultants don't get tipped, not even when they provide good service. Coming from Europe, tipping isn't all that common to begin with, so my first introduction to the concept was when I started to travel to North America more, beginning with New York. I was pleasantly surprised with the level of service in restaurants. I had been used to prompt service, sometimes bordering on being rude. The European waiters and waitresses weren't expecting to be tipped to begin with, while still collecting a decent wage.

When I first came to Manhattan, my travel guide book informed me that wait staff works for minimum wage or even less, and rely on tips to be able to pay their bills. I came mentally prepared to pay at least fifteen percent on top of my restaurant bills, and was pleasantly surprised that in exchange for that I didn't only get better service than I had been used to before, I also got free water, bread, refills on drinks, and sometimes even a small appetizer or dessert with my meal. Something I wasn't used to in Europe, where I paid for every single glass of tap water that was served as if it was mineral water. North American wait staff wasn't just expecting to be tipped out of custom, most of them were actually trying to get a bigger tip by providing excellent service.

Imagine my surprise when one of my business clients took me out for lunch to an excellent, upscale Japanese restaurant in midtown Manhattan. The lunch was paid for in cash, and I couldn't help but notice that hardly any tip was left. The amount was rounded up to the nearest five-dollar amount, but that was it. My client must have noticed a slightly puzzled look on my face, and responded to my unspoken question with a smile, and "Tipping is for tourists."

So it begs the question - is there a conspiracy between guide book authors and the software that prints receipts in restaurants that say "a 15-20% tip is customary in North America"? I don't know. And honestly I don't care. I've grown accustomed to the North American standards when it comes to wait staff, who are generally very friendly and take excellent care of me while dining out. I have no problem rewarding them directly for that. I also have no problem leaving zero tip for bad or below average service - there has been a few occasions where I deemed that appropriate. What goes around comes around.

Where to buy memories

S ouvenir shops are inevitable. You'll find them anywhere, even when you least expect it. They all cater to a never-ending stream of tourists. Their entire business model is based on the simple fact that people want to take memories and keepsakes from their trip home. Even the most budget conscious traveler has a set (minimum) amount of money that's burning in their pocket, waiting to be spent on something tacky. If traveling to a country with a different currency this "problem" is amplified since changing currency back after coming home is even more expensive than taking out foreign currency in the first place. An entire industry exists thanks to this - lots of "local" businesses at the destination are willing to help you get rid of your spending money in exchange for experiences (excursions) or "authentic" souvenirs, most of which are made in China.

When it comes to shopping and spending money while traveling I'm no different. I want to undergo as many experiences as possible (more about excursions later) and submerse myself in the culture of my new surroundings. Just like all other travellers, I also want to bring home something tangible to remind me of another memorable trip. For a long time I took shelter in some of those large "made in China" souvenir shops and brought many collectibles home. What I brought home wasn't all that much different from what any other tourist hauled back to the airport. Especially since baggage rules have intensified to a point where there's almost no way to travel without paying over-weight charges anymore, I decided to do things a little different. If I'm paying for my luggage anyway I might as well regard that money as an "investment" to bring home something truly unique. Although I have my fair share of "I love New York" T-shirts, sweaters, mugs and other memorabilia, I now set out to buy something more useful instead. While it's easy to spend a small fortune in New York, I've learned that if I'm willing to look around a little, it can be *cheaper* to buy designer clothing. Unlike my "I love New York" shirt, I can wear those clothes

> *"Though we travel the world over to find the beautiful, we must carry it with us or we find it not."*
>
> Ralph Waldo Emerson

almost everyday, even when I go to work or visit a client. In most corporate offices wearing T-shirts, in particular "I love New York" shirts, is frowned upon (my take

on corporate culture is something I might cover in a future book). I now fly home with practical clothes I can use everyday. They function to me as the perfect memory of a trip. And I didn't have to venture too far off the beaten path: to stick with the New York example I've had some excellent finds in a few of the flagship stores on Park and Fifth Avenue. In case you're not familiar with Manhattan, those two streets are perceived as where one might go bankrupt on a single small shopping spree. While this holds true to some extent, there's some great finds to be had. The experience of shopping for my version of memorabilia that way is, at least in my opinion, a lot more pleasant than hanging out in crowded, busy souvenir shops.

In Buenos Aires I took a different approach. While there's some amazing shopping in that city, I discovered that, thanks to the weaker Argentine peso, prices where adjusted to meet the stronger US Dollar in most of the main street stores on Florida. Usually I'm not a big fan of street vendors due to the higher-than-normal odds of being ripped off, however in this city there was an abundance of market style vendors that had set up a small booth or table to sell their, often handmade, products. Much to my surprise, prices turned out to be less than half or sometimes a quarter of what was charged in main street stores. In exchange I got to take home handmade products by local artists instead of mass produced items. It was my first visit to this amazing city, so of course I had to take home some tacky touristy stuff in addition to my local finds. The majority of my pesos was spent on treasures I found at local markets, buying directly from the people who made the item. While my mass produced "Buenos Aires" sweater definitely is one of my favorite sweaters to wear on a cold Canadian winter day, I'm most happy with my hand made, hand painted treasures that are truly unique to me and tell a much better story of the character of the city.

Take pictures or make photographs

Full disclosure: I'm a professional photographer, so I'm a bit opinionated when it comes to taking pictures, in particular travel photography. There are plenty of, sometimes useful, books already written that attempt to help you get the most out of your camera and take the best travel snapshots possible. Buy some and keep the ones that help you. I'm not going to discourage you from taking pictures. Actually I would encourage anyone to take amazing photographs, preferably better than mine. Contrary to what people believe there is very little competition in photography. We all have our unique view of the world, and there are an unlimited number of viewpoints a person can take to view the world from. Recreating an image that someone else took (or sometimes millions of others have already taken) is in most cases relatively easy. A quick search online will show some amazing pictures of the Eiffel Tower, and most of them look very similar. I still take the "traditional" Eiffel tower picture every time I visit Paris (or Las Vegas). However the second Eiffel Tower picture I take, I'll always take from an uncommon viewpoint. I might crawl on all fours over the pavement, looking up at the tower to create a different composition. On the other end of the spectrum, I might charter a helicopter to fly over the tower and get an aerial view instead. The opportunities are endless, and even the most common landmarks still have many unique angles that haven't been explored yet. The challenge is to find one that works. Be crazy, be creative, and try something unique. Thanks to the digital cameras there is no risk of wasting expensive film anymore. So shoot away, and have some fun.

But wait... before you start: pause, and think about what you're doing. I'm having a hard time watching people take a constant stream of pictures on their tablets or phones from a sightseeing bus. Admitted, smart phones and tablets come equipped with some decent cameras these days. Some of them do an above average job of capturing the vacation snapshots. Still, I find that when I'm stuck sitting on a sightseeing bus I'm missing out on a lot of the experiences my destination has to offer. If I'm attempting to get some good pictures I find the space I have on a (moving) bus to be very limited, so trying to find a unique viewpoint becomes extremely challenging. Or I might miss the moment completely since the bus (or, in case of Paris, sightseeing boat) already moved on. Taking good pictures takes time, a lot of time. So instead of snapping away and coming home with thousands of pictures spread out over multiple memory cards, I set myself a goal. What am I going to do with those pictures when I come home?

Being a travel photographer my goal is two-fold: I mainly take pictures for myself of anything that somehow left an impression while I was traveling. That way I come home with some pictures that tell a personal story of my trip, and I usually end up printing and framing some of my work for my own enjoyment. The second goal is to fund my next adventure by selling some of my work as photographic art. To do that I need to ensure I come home with some truly unique viewpoints that people will love

> *"We don't take pictures with our cameras; we take them with our hearts and minds."*
>
> *Arnold Newman*

enough they'll want it on their own walls. Not everyone who enjoys traveling is as dedicated to (read: obsessed with) photography as I am while traveling. Finding some unique point of view takes a lot of time and effort. I notice more and more people choose to take very little pictures while they are travelling, and instead opt to buy the work of a travel photographer like myself from the place they visited. I'm fine either way.

Tourists and Travelers

If you picked up this book you're probably not the tour bus type person. But even if you are, I'm not judging. I've been on a few organized tours and excursions myself. I've had some really good experiences doing so. I've also had a few really, really bad experiences. One noteworthy example was a jeep safari on one of the Spanish islands. After being shuttled to another town from where the actual departure took place, it took less than fifteen minutes until the first stop. The location for this first stop was an isolated, dry, sandy parking lot. Everyone left the jeeps wondering why a stop was made, since we were in a location far from anything scenic, but far enough from town to make it impossible to escape the tour and run back to civilization. When the next thirty to sixty minutes were spend taking photographs of every participant of the tour, followed by selling overpriced merchandise as a "keepsake", I did seriously consider running. I didn't, hoping things would get better as the day progressed. The second stop was a very early lunch break at about 10am at an overpriced, otherwise empty street side restaurant. The remainder of the day was a bit more interesting, but my experience was already ruined by the horrible start of the "safari". I would not recommend anyone to ever sign up for anything called a "jeep safari", unless you're in Africa.

On my next trip to another tropical island I rented a 4x4 jeep myself and ran my own, private jeep safari experience. Maybe not the safest option, but I figured it would be hard to get lost on a relatively small island. I do want to apologize to the car rental company for bringing the vehicle back so dirty, and completely missing the "no off road use" clause in the rental agreement. Honestly, I didn't realize that until later. Regardless, that self-guided trip was a lot more fun, partially because there were no pushy sales people anywhere in sight. By now it's safe to say I'm a "do it yourself" kind of person when it comes to exploring. I do my research, and based on my list of things to do I'll venture out to go see most of what I want to see on my own. For most of those, a tour guide of any sorts is really not necessary. Even when I'm not familiar with a destination I usually just roam a few blocks around my hotel aimlessly to make myself familiar, and then on subsequent days attempt a self-guided walking tour or two, to explore a bit further. Those self-guided walks are a great way to find hidden gems that I wouldn't have necessarily found on my own, without the guide book. In a way I'm like a cat that is let out of the house for the first time. At first they're a little scared and tend to run back to the safety of the house, but as the hours and days progress it'll stray further and further, getting more excited about the adventures the day will bring.

Most cities offer the famous double-decker sightseeing tours, which can be a great way to easily see some major landmarks. Typically I avoid those buses, however. They always include a number of stops that I'm not interested in and while most bus operators (but not all) will allow you to skip those stops, I still find it a waste of time to actually have to travel to, and then past them. Public transit, especially subways, are my chosen form of transportation whenever available. Tokyo, Paris, London, New York, and many more metropolitan areas have a very tight and well-serviced network that gets me to my destinations in a (mostly) safe and (always) cheap manner. It takes a little studying of the maps and subway stations, but in return I get much greater flexibility compared to the scheduled tourist buses. Most cities offer unlimited ride cards for one or multiple days, which provide even more value.

The one exception where I did end up taking a scheduled tourist bus was in Buenos Aires. I was planning to visit the neighborhood of "La Boca" which is known for its remarkable, colorful buildings. I still don't know if it's really true, but multiple people as well as my guidebook recommended against my plan of going there on my own. I usually take advice like that with a grain of salt. I'm always aware of my surroundings and take the necessary precautions to be safe, no matter where I am. In most places that common sense thinking gets me around safely. Not in

> *"The traveler sees what he sees, the tourist sees what he has come to see."*
>
> Gilbert K. Chesterson

La Boca, so I've been told. While the general touristy area of La Boca is pretty safe and a spot not to be missed, getting in and out of the area can be a little tricky as there are some less popular areas in the immediate vicinity. Others, including numerous locals, have described those areas to me as being just plain dangerous. Better safe than sorry, so I decided to go against my no-bus rule and buy a ticket for one of those bright yellow sightseeing buses. Being pretty well known and quite touristy, La Boca was one of their stops. I reasoned that if the surrounding areas were a little (or a lot, depending on who I talked to) unsafe, a bright yellow tourist bus with many other people on it was probably my best bet to get in unharmed. While this simplistic theory might not always work, it did for me. I got safely in (and out) of the La Boca area and was able to explore some of the typical colorful streets on my own. More importantly, I felt completely safe doing so. All other areas of Buenos Aires I explored more or less successful by public transit, since the city actually has a pretty good subway system. Other than almost getting mugged once (being a photographer I can't always keep my camera and lenses hidden...) I had no issues whatsoever.

Another time when organized tourism comes in handy is when it's simply not safe to go on my own at all. In those cases I'll submit myself to undergo the tourist experience by being shuttled around between collection and drop-off points. Not that I enjoy that experience per se, but the end result is worth it. In the Philippines, I had to embark on a multi-hour shuttle van ride, and then transfer to a tiny boat to get to a particular destination. At every embarkation and disembarkation point the group was swarmed with extremely pushy street vendors who had no sense of personal space or setting a reasonably fair price for their products. The objective of that day however made up for it: to go and explore an underground river, one of the 7 wonders of nature. This fact does depend on which list you choose to use for the "7 wonders", as there are a couple of variations of this list available. I'll admit it was a very impressive experience. Just picture the surroundings - you're in pitch black, thick humid air. Other than a battery operated lamp on front of the boat, which attracts the most interesting flying creatures, there's no light whatsoever. Numerous poisonous snakes and spiders inhabit the caves, and trying to avoid those is key to a successful return out the complete darkness. I sure was happy hearing the reassuring chatter of the talkative tour guide from the back of the boat. He explained we were only allowed to go into the underground river for a certain distance, as beyond those boundaries special gear and certifications were required to deal with the poisonous spiders and snakes. I could only hope those creatures would abide by the same certification requirements and stick to their side of the river.

Exploring one of the seven world wonders was an experience not to be missed, and definitely worth being hassled a bit on the way there. It was also something not to be attempted on my own, and I'm happy I didn't. A rule of thumb for me is to limit these types of excursions. There's no need to have a jam-packed itinerary and have an activity pre-booked and scheduled for every single hour in the day. If available, to embark on an experience like an underground river is something worthwhile, but one of these things every few days is definitely enough for me. It's all about finding a balance between doing things on my own, and undergoing an experience that requires me to buy a ticket. Generally speaking, I think it's safe to conclude that whenever the conditions aren't of any extreme or dangerous nature, I'd much rather explore on my own and take a side road here and there to soak in everything a destination has to offer. Provided the snakes and spiders stay on their side of the road.

A safe and happy day

Since GPS units don't come with an "avoid bad areas" option, people tend to get a bit concerned about their personal safety while traveling. I've traveled a lot solo, which is, sadly enough, still easier for a guy than for my fellow female world travellers. Being emancipated as I am I think that's a sad reality, but one we have to deal with and keep in mind nonetheless. Having the tall European genes probably helps a bit too in keeping me safe. Regardless of genes and gender, there are some rules that I think would benefit all in staying safe, and maybe even making the world in general a little bit of a safer place for everyone.

My most important rule, no matter where I am, is to be *aware* of my surroundings. The less I appear to be a tourist, the safer I am. It appears that most crimes that involve tourists occur right in the tourist areas, in particular airports, hotels, and major sightseeing spots. If I can be more "at home" while traveling and act like the locals do, I'm automatically safer no matter where in the world I find myself next. When I'm aware of what's happening around me, I can anticipate to whatever is happening, and choose to change my path if I wanted or needed to. Anticipation works wonders when participating in traffic too by the way. Be aware of what's happening and react to it appropriately, in a timely fashion, to avoid accidents. The same applies when navigating an unfamiliar city or destination. Know what's happening around you, and if you see something you don't trust, change your path.

Statistics show that some Canadian cities are amongst the safest in the world - and I'm proud to enjoy the privilege of living in one. Despite this wonderful statistic about the city I now call home, I know that there are certain areas one should try to avoid, especially during nighttime. This applies to every city in the world. They all have bad spots one should avoid, although some more than others. If I'm visiting as a tourist, there's very little to see there anyway. And even if there is, it might not be worth the risk. I learned this the hard way by looking for some photogenic spots in Brooklyn, New York. I like to wander around and get a little lost at times, which usually results in finding some great spots off the beaten track. In Brooklyn it caused me to get lost in the Projects, a less favorable area of town. I recognized the buildings from shows like CSI, and knew I wasn't where I intended or even wanted to be. I got some weird looks from people who also questioned my need or desire to be where I was, but I just kept walking and tried not to look like I was lost, which I know would have made me an even easier target for trouble. Everything worked out fine and I made it out of there safe and sound, with an experience richer.

Stubborn as I am, the next day I decided to visit Harlem, which, according to my travel book was "a lot safer than it used to be". I'm sure it was, and nothing significant happened, however I noticed how shortly after I stepped out of the subway station a police officer started following me, while keeping a distance of about half a block. I must have looked out of place with my camera gear, I suppose. While roaming around the area, I did find a fantastic local market and picked up some unique souvenirs, all whilst being closely watched by the police officer from a short distance. I still believe my guide book was right in saying Harlem is safer than it used to be, but then again in most areas

I've visited around the globe I don't get a police tail to make sure I'm safe. Thanks, NYPD!

One time I wished I had a police escort was in the Buenos Aires subway - the train was very crowded and I felt uncomfortable somehow, when an older man who attempted to appear drunk bumped into me. Meanwhile someone from behind tried to take my iPhone out of my pocket. Sadly for these two gentlemen I take my rule to be aware of my surroundings very seriously, even in crowded trains. I instantly felt the unauthorized movement in my pocket. I turned, pushed my way out of the crowd and moved to the other side of the train. I was still in possession of my phone, camera and wallet. They got off at the next station, and I continued on my way back to my hotel. Does that make South America, like so many have told me, an unsafe place to be? I don't think so. The same thing could have happened to me anywhere else in the world, including my "safe" hometown. Crime rates are just statistics, and if I'm the victim of a crime it doesn't matter to me whether I'm part of a 10% or 25% statistic. Statistics are meaningless when dealing with individuals. Crime happens even in the safest of places, and the best prevention is to keep belongings safe and be aware of what's happening around you at all times, anticipating to every situation and changing your way if needed. The main thing is to plan ahead and know what areas to avoid - getting lost in bad areas of town isn't something I would recommend to anyone. That day could have ended differently, but thanks to a combination of luck, common sense and quite possibly tall European genes it didn't.

Cost per minute

Although there are certain travel secrets that will definitely help keep the cost under control, travel is not necessarily a cheap way to spend time. Staying at home on the couch is in most circumstances (though not always) a cheaper alternative compared to exploring the corners of our planet. For this reason I roughly calculate the cost per minute of my trip before departure. Taking everything into consideration, from flights, to accommodation, transportation and potentially missed or delayed income at home - the cost per minute of traveling is usually more than just a few pennies. However, this chapter is not intended to deter you from traveling. Quite the contrary. Instead of mourning the "loss" of money, I've learned to use my cost per minute as a *motivator* to maximize the value I get out of the experience of travel. And as a result, sometimes I spent even more, or opted for a better type of accommodation or mode of transportation.

I've made it one of my principles to always fly direct whenever possible. While this is in most cases a more expensive option than going for one, or even multiple stopovers in different airports, it's always the fastest way to get to my destination. Although I like drinking coffee at 30,000 feet, I'd like to avoid the additional hassle and stress by adding unnecessary airports and stopovers to the mix. Not even to mention the risk of missing connections, or my luggage getting lost somewhere along the way. The slightly higher cost of flying direct mitigates most of those risks, and more importantly it buys me at least a few extra hours on the beach, or more time to explore a new and different country, city and culture.

With the high cost per minute of the entire trip, it's definitely worth it to splurge every once in a while on things that add to the experience value of the journey. It also makes me conscious in decisions I make: the cost of being here in this very minute is substantial, so it is my moral imperative to make the most of the Experience Value I take out of it.

Don't do it

Experiences can be good or bad, and one of the worst things to deal with while traveling is a bad experience. Being pretty self-supporting I enjoy figuring things out on my own. On top of that I think I also have a problem with authority, so anyone telling me what to do will, to some extent, upset me. The combination of these two traits will lead me to steer away as far as possible from many forms of organized tourism. I'm referring to the kind where I'm required to embark on some mode of group transportation, like a bus, and I'm being told when to get off and how much time I'll have to "quickly" take photographs. I've had some unpleasant experiences with these types of tours in the past. In Singapore I was rushed in and out of places along the route that were supposed to be interesting. Nothing was further from the truth. Most of the "interesting" places were jewelry and souvenir stores. It made me wonder how much those stores paid the tour company for a fresh bus load of tourists every day. To call it a tourist trap would be an understatement, and from the five or so stops on the trip there was only one that was worth paying a visit. To make matters worse this place was only a five-minute taxi ride from the hotel. From the little time I had in Singapore, unfortunately an entire day was wasted on this "city tour".

> *"Never go on trips with anyone you do not love"*
>
> Ernest Hemingway

This particular city tour turned into a negative Experience Value for me - roaming the streets and exploring on my own would have been much more rewarding. My motto now is - when in doubt, don't do it. I know I'm able to enjoy myself roaming the streets and discovering new places every day. There's no need to hop on (or off) any sort of excursion to accomplish the same thing. This of course all depends on my personal level of comfort and sense of adventure - one person will attempt more on their own than others. Then again, if you were the type of traveler who prefers to take pictures on a tablet camera from the top deck of a tour bus without even getting off, you probably wouldn't have picked up this book to begin with.

COME HOME

WHY IS OUR TRAVELING SELF
SO DIFFERENT FROM OUR "HOME" SELF?

Where does your trip take you?

My trip to Buenos Aires has shown me the mentality of the people there is so warm, friendly, and *passionate* about life. I just had to adopt a piece of that in my own lifestyle somehow. Those who know me personally know that I do tend to be very passionate, especially when things don't work out the way I had envisioned them. Some have called me impatient or grumpy, but I prefer the "passionate" explanation.

The idea for this book was born in Asia, where I finally realized that some of the principles I apply to travel could be of service to much more people than just me and the people I travel with. But in the end the question "where does your trip take you" doesn't have much to do with the *physical* destination. It's all about where travel takes me in life. What part of my next trip will I take home with me that helps me grow in my daily life? I usually don't know until I get there what I was looking for. All the more reason to travel, and find out.

> *"Life isn't about finding yourself. Life is about creating yourself."*
>
> George Bernard Shaw

Culture Shock

Culture shock is a topic I want to briefly touch upon. An entire library could be written about this interesting side effect of travel. I've experienced culture shock in many different ways, and as long as you venture far enough off the beaten path it's bound to happen at some point. Often culture shock is nothing too serious; it's just a reaction of surprise to something the mind is not familiar with. The first time I encountered hunting rifles and handguns out in the open in some sports equipment store in the US could be called somewhat of a "culture shock" for me. Being originally from Europe that image was just not something I was familiar with. Sure enough, I knew about the firearms policies of the US and while I don't have a strong opinion on the matter, seeing it out there in plain daylight just made me pause for a brief second. Like it suddenly hit me, "this is different".

The same thing happened when I first encountered a grizzly bear after moving to Canada. I knew they live here, and I always made sure my hiking trips in the beautiful Rocky Mountains were prepared and "bear aware". I even carried bear spray, just in case. And yet seeing one for the first time made me pause again for a split second when it finally hit me - "they actually *do* live here!".

This kind of "culture shock" is insignificant and fairly innocent, more a sudden realization of something I was already aware of, but just hadn't experienced with my own eyes yet. Some culture shock experiences go a bit deeper than that, however. The first time I got to experience that kind of culture shock was in the first year after relocating to Canada. Even though Canada is a Western country, which on many counts is very similar to Europe, there are slight differences. An excellent read on the topic of Canadian culture is "How to be a Canadian" or "Why I hate Canadians", both titles from Canadian author Will Ferguson. I read both books in addition to many others before making my move, and considered myself well prepared. I still think my preparation was solid, but nothing could have prepared me for the deep uncomfortable feeling of being completely removed from anything I had

> *"Every experience, no matter how bad it seems, holds within it a blessing of some kind. The goal is to find it."*
>
> *Unknown*

considered to be familiar. In some way it was a very liberating experience for me, dealing with life's issues and forcing me to eventually redefine and rebuild my life from scratch.

Dealing with issues through traveling

There's an upside to culture shock. I used this psychological effect as a trigger to deal with some significant issues in my life, and in myself. When something shocking happens in my day-to-day life, or I just get overwhelmed with it all, I often resort to travel to find a different perspective. Sometimes I might even find a solution. Some might perceive it as running away from issues, but the one thing I've learned is that you're not able to leave everything behind that easily. No matter how many material possessions, circumstances, friends or family I left behind temporarily or permanently, I always ended up taking the one thing with me that I could not leave behind: *myself*.

Sometimes running away, or taking a break from it all, was the only thing I saw left to do. I would simply book a ticket to some remote location and spend a couple of days, or sometimes weeks, roaming the streets of some unfamiliar place. Skiing the French and Swiss Alps worked great, too. By removing all daily routines and distractions I was left with just myself. Nobody else to talk to, just myself to work things out. It turned out to be the greatest kick starter to resolve my life's issues and become myself again. Travel

> *"One travels more usefully when alone, because he reflects more."*
>
> Thomas Jefferson

ended up to be a catalyst for personal growth. "If you can make it there, you can make it anywhere." It is what they say about New York City, but I think it applies to any unfamiliar place. Coincidentally, if you choose to believe in coincidences, New York was the first city across the Atlantic Ocean I visited in my life. And, I figured, since I made it there, maybe I could make it anywhere. My reasoning was based on my small victories: I had worked in Manhattan for a while, and managed to find something to eat everyday, not go hungry and stay alive. "I made it there, I *can* make it anywhere", I promised myself.

I ended up traveling more and more; removing myself further and further from everything I was familiar with. I put myself in new environments, new cultures, and even new languages every time. The only constant was me, the person undertaking the journey. I faced a lot of fears. My fear of heights, fear of being alone and in general a fear of the unknown. The heights are easy to deal with - there are many towers and viewpoints that I just had to see. And, since I'm an avid skier, riding some scary chair lift to the top of the mountain turned out to be the only way for me to be able to enjoy the ride down. The fear of being alone had a much bigger impact. Nothing could prepare me for the shock of moving across the Atlantic Ocean, ending up in more or less unfamiliar territory all by myself. No friends, no family, no one to turn to. It's been an unbelievable confrontational experience, where life held up a different mirror every day about who I thought I really was.

Everything looks better in black and white, and in hindsight everything seems so much easier. All those fears got resolved and dissolved quickly. The only thing to do is go out there, meet people, and make new friends - and family. That in itself deals with the fear of the unknown at the same time. The only way is to go out, and explore. Make unfamiliar territory familiar. Unlike loneliness, being alone isn't such a bad thing every once in a while. It gives time to reflect, think about what's truly important to me as a human being. What are the things that I want out of this life, and where am I going next - both literally and figuratively speaking? It's a hell of a ride if you commit to it, but worth every second and every penny you invest in it. It turns out to be a time and money thing, after all.

Home stays behind

It's never been easier to stay in touch with "home" while traveling these days. Internet, email, and even cheaper roaming deals for my cellphone make it relatively easy to stay in touch. Assuming I'm more or less in the same time zone, otherwise a little planning is required. This has proven to be very valuable for me, as it allows me to work no matter where in the world I am. I've booked and confirmed photography and art shows while exploring Asia all thanks to the blessing of virtual phone lines and email. Especially on trips that span over multiple weeks or months staying in touch with home has become a necessity to me. It's a great learning experience, too. I really didn't want to work all that much while traveling. I merely wanted to keep the momentum going, and maybe initiate a new idea that came to mind. After a few days when I put myself in different surroundings, my mind operates differently. I want to deal with "work" related activities quickly and effectively, and get on with my day. To me doing this daily over my morning coffee from Manila has shown me new ways to run my business. Dealing with an inbox full of unnecessary clutter is a big hassle when all I wanted to do was to get out of the door and explore all the new things the world had to offer. Also, broadband, "high speed" internet in Manila turned out to be closer to dial up speed at best, and that was on the good days. So I set up rules in both my inbox and my mind to only deal with anything that proved to be of immediate business value. In my case that was either a direct sale, booking, or opportunity for an event within the first two months after coming home. With Christmas coming up soon, there were a lot of Christmas events and markets I was trying to get into, so planning ahead for those was the main portion of my work every day. I simply couldn't wait until I was home to deal with all of those opportunities, since events fill up quickly and I didn't want to be left out of the busy Christmas season. Reducing unnecessary clutter from my day-to-day operations was a great exercise in learning to focus on what's truly important. At home, how much time didn't I waste on tasks that weren't all that important anyway? What part of my activities actually result in direct business value for my company? A lot of the *stuff* we do is waste, to more or less fill the customary forty hours of mandatory attendance at the office. Even after leaving the corporate world and starting my own company, I still find it hard to not obey the forty-hour expectation. Just taking a day off on any random day like a Tuesday when I really need to take a break, is something I struggle with, even now I'm my own "boss". The mind is a funny thing.

In the Philippines, I was removed from all of those expectations. I was put into a culture halfway around the world I wasn't familiar with. On top of that I had to work in a time zone that reduced the number of "connectable" hours, where I could interact with my home base in North America, to only a few hours every day. It made many things a lot less important. If there were only one or two hours where I could talk to people back home, that's the time I limited myself to use for work, even though most of my interactions were indirect via email. Having little available time (and unreliable internet) forced me to prioritize my activities and only deal with anything that required my immediate attention and would lead to direct results. For me and most other companies and entrepreneurs out there, that meant sales, or the opportunity to sell. Money going into my bank account. Anything else, I told myself, I would deal with after I came home. It turned out I never ended up dealing with those items that were left for later. Most of it seemed important enough to not be deleted right away at the time, but it really wasn't that important after all. Even problems that looked like they were critical, resolved themselves nine out of ten times. This is one of the biggest lessons I took home from that trip. And even things that seem important and do need some attention, usually need less attention than it appears. I remember one art event where the organizer required my commitment to participate. The event was scheduled to happen shortly after I came back. My commitment I could easily confirm via email. Except there was a deadline of less than one week where my participation also had to be confirmed with a cheque for payment of rent for my space. The cheque had to be sent in, physically, via actual mail. Now while I can email signed PDF documents, and electronically transfer money even when I'm on the other side of the world, doing those things on paper by regular mail is simply not going to happen unless I was willing to spend a small fortune on overnight courier services. Something I wasn't prepared to do. As a matter of fact the whole deadline meant very little to me. While this was an event I really wanted to participate in, it was absolutely clear to me the deadline was just some arbitrary day that had very little to do with my commitment to participate. So I sent an email to the organizers that I was happy to take part, but would deal with the paperwork immediately upon my return from Asia. They accepted, and never asked for the physical paperwork to be completed, other than payment for the space.

This experience has shown me that a lot of "deadlines" and "processes that *must* be followed" I have grown accustomed to, are completely arbitrary. With a long work history in business process consult-ing I still do believe some level of standardization is a great thing, but as a society we've taken that to an extreme level where it serves no purpose whatsoever anymore. Coming to this realization has taught me to say "no" more often, and I don't always comply with requests or processes I don't believe in. Especially when nobody is even able to explain why we're doing things the way we do them, or what purpose they serve, in the first place. I'm sure I've annoyed some people with this mindset. Please accept my sincere apology for any grievance I've caused. I hope I've been able to at least explain why I do things the way I do.

In the end staying in touch with limited time, and an even more limited Internet connection has proven to be of great value. It contin-ues to benefit me even after coming home. Still, while I'm traveling I prefer to completely disconnect for a while if I can. Taking myself away from day-to-day life and daily operations has become an automatic brainstorming exercise where my mind is free to come up with all sort of new ideas I can put into action once I come home, or sometimes even while I'm still traveling. I tend to just write a few short notes to act on once I get home, or I'll even send out an email or two to get the ball rolling on whatever new idea crossed my mind. Like with all ideas, some work out, some don't. Being able to get the ball rolling made staying in touch sort of a necessary evil to me. When I'm on shorter trips, like a few short weeks in Hawaii, I prefer to cut all ties temporarily and completely disconnect to let my mind and body relax and reset. The value in fresh ideas and motivation I take home after being off the grid for a while is typically much larger.

Freedom

W hy is our traveling self so different from our "home" self? I love the experience of travel for the benefits and opportunities it offers. Travel is an opportunity to grow, and learn new things, both about myself and about the world. Yet for many years, every time when I came home, I surrendered myself quickly to my daily life. I would go back to work, sit in my cubicle from nine to five (or so), and save up for the next adventure. There's nothing wrong with that lifestyle and I more or less enjoyed it for a long time. But why is it I feel so much more alive, and enjoy a bigger sense of freedom while on a journey than when I am at home? Am I using travel as an escape mechanism to get away from a life I didn't want to live in the first place? If so, would it be possible to take that sensation of freedom home with me - and live my entire life that way? I would still go travel, but not *need* to travel anymore to temporarily escape from my life.

I think it's possible. Living life with the idea that "tomorrow will be better" is a lie. Yet that's how we're raised. Starting at a young age we go to school, high school, college or university, all to obtain a good job at a solid company to build a life. And once we're there, we're working long hours for an opportunity to climb the corporate ladder and advance ourselves in a career we might not even like. But it's all good, because it helps pay the bills, especially the bills from the travel agency for the next trip we will undertake. Because that's what life is all about, right? I lived my life that way, for a very long time. Striving, and working very hard to get to the next big thing. And by the time you get to the next big thing, there would be another next big thing one step ahead of me on the ladder of life, corporate ladder, or both; always climbing, always trying to get ahead.

What happened to taking a real break every once in a while? Instead of climbing, I now choose to look around - enjoy the altitude I am at right now. The view is *spectacular*. I breathe in the fresh air, and think about whether I should climb up another level. I probably can - but I don't *have* to anymore. Things are pretty good as they are today. After many years of traveling and dealing with my life's issues while away from home, I'm learning to live a life I enjoy right where I live. That's the true

> *"We shall not cease from exploration, and the end of all our exploring will be to arrive where we started and know the place for the first time."*
>
> T.S. Eliot

message of the Freedom Project. It is to take all the principles from this book like *Experience Value* and *Small Victories* home with you, to apply to your daily life.

We already knew that travel isn't about the destination - it's about the journey. The same applies to life. Life is not about the next destination - it's about the journey of life as a whole. And life is at home - wherever that may be for you. That journey doesn't start in the departure lounge of some airport - it starts when you come home, unpack, do the laundry and wake up refreshed for another day. In the end, home is not a place, it's a feeling. Bon voyage!

Parting words

Moments (Spanish: 'Instantes') is the title of a poem that's often incorrectly attributed to Argentine writer Jorge Luis Borges. The poem has become very popular thanks to numerous books, articles, and even email chain letters. The original author remains unknown.

I'm including these inspiring words at the end of my book as it shows most regrets are for things we didn't end up doing. Embrace the unknown.

Moments

If I could live again my life,

In the next – I'll try,

- to make more mistakes,

I won't try to be so perfect,

I'll be more relaxed,

I'll be more full – than I am now,

In fact, I'll take fewer things seriously,

I'll be less hygienic,

I'll take more risks,

I'll take more trips,

I'll watch more sunsets,

I'll climb more mountains,

I'll swim more rivers,

I'll go to more places – I've never been,

I'll eat more ice creams and less (lime) beans,

I'll have more real problems – and less imaginary ones,

I was one of those people who live

prudent and prolific lives -

each minute of his life,

Of course that I had moments of joy – but,

if I could go back I'll try to have only good moments,

If you don't know – that's what life is made of,

Don't lose the now!

I was one of those who never goes anywhere

without a thermometer,

without a hot-water bottle,

and without an umbrella and without a parachute,

If I could live again – I will travel light,

If I could live again – I'll try to work bare feet

at the beginning of spring till the end of autumn,

I'll ride more carts,

I'll watch more sunrises and play with more children,

If I have the life to live – but now I am 85,

- and I know that I am dying ...

About the author

Wilko is a self taught, professional photographer and photographic artist. He has been capturing our wonderful planet, and it's beautiful inhabitants, for more than half his life. Through his art, writing and appearances as a keynote speaker he enjoys sharing his colorful experiences with the public.

Wilko was born in the Netherlands, and currently lives in Calgary, Canada. His inspiration comes from traveling all over the world: he calls the Rocky Mountains his "home", and rest of the world his "office". Visit him online at **www.wilko.ca**.

"I fell in love with the exceptional things I saw and the remarkable people who crossed my path."

Wilko van de Kamp

20820244R00101

Made in the USA
San Bernardino, CA
25 April 2015